HOW TO WRITE YOUR OWN PREMARITAL AGREEMENT

HOW TO WRITE YOUR OWN PREMARITAL AGREEMENT

with forms

Edward A. Haman
Attorney at Law

Sphinx® Publishing
A Division of Sourcebooks, Inc.
Naperville, IL • Clearwater, FL

Second Edition, 1998

Published by: **Sphinx® Publishing, A Division of Sourcebooks, Inc.**

Sourcebooks Office
P.O. Box 372
Naperville, Illinois 60566
(630) 961-3900
FAX: 630-961-2168

Sphinx Publishing Office
P.O. Box 25
Clearwater, Florida 33757
(813) 587-0999
FAX: 813-586-5088

Cover Design: Andrew Sardina/Dominique Raccah, Sourcebooks, Inc.
Interior Design and Production: Andrew Sardina, Sourcebooks, Inc.

This publication is designed to provide accurate and authoritative information in regard to the subject matter covered. It is sold with the understanding that the publisher is not engaged in rendering legal, accounting, or other professional service. If legal advice or other expert assistance is required, the services of a competent professional person should be sought.

From a Declaration of Principles Jointly Adopted by a Committee of the
American Bar Association and a Committee of Publishers and Associations

Library of Congress Cataloging-in-Publication Data
Haman, Edward A.
    How to write your own premarital agreement : with forms / Edward
A. Haman.—2nd ed.
        p.   cm.
Includes index.
    ISBN 1-57071-344-8 (pbk.)
    1. Antenuptial contracts—United States—Popular works.
2. Antenuptial contracts—United States—Forms.   I. Title.
KF529.Z9H35   1998
346.7301'6—dc21
                                                                98-13665
                                                                CIP

Printed and bound in the United States of America.

Paperback — 10 9 8 7 6 5 4 3 2 1

CONTENTS

USING SELF-HELP LAW BOOKS

Whenever you shop for a product or service, you are faced with various levels of quality and price. In deciding what product or service to buy, you make a cost/value analysis on the basis of your willingness to pay and the quality you desire.

When buying a car, you decide whether you want transportation, comfort, status, or sex appeal. Accordingly, you decide among such choices as a Neon, a Lincoln, a Rolls Royce, or a Porsche. Before making a decision, you usually weigh the merits of each option against the cost.

When you get a headache, you can take a pain reliever (such as aspirin) or visit a medical specialist for a neurological examination. Given this choice, most people, of course, take a pain reliever, since it costs only pennies, whereas a medical examination costs hundreds of dollars and takes a lot of time. This is usually a logical choice because rarely is anything more than a pain reliever needed for a headache. But in some cases, a headache may indicate a brain tumor, and failing to see a specialist right away can result in complications. Should everyone with a headache go to a specialist? Of course not, but people treating their own illnesses must realize that they are betting on the basis of their cost/value analysis of the situation, they are taking the most logical option.

The same cost/value analysis must be made in deciding to do one's own legal work. Many legal situations are very straight forward, requiring a simple form and no complicated analysis. Anyone with a little intelligence and a book of instructions can handle the matter without outside help.

But there is always the chance that complications are involved that only an attorney would notice. To simplify the law into a book like this, several legal cases often must be condensed into a single sentence or paragraph. Otherwise, the book would be several hundred pages long and too complicated for most people. However, this simplification necessarily leaves out many details and nuances that would apply to special or unusual situations. Also, there are many ways to interpret most legal questions. Your case may come before a judge who disagrees with the analysis of our authors.

Therefore, in deciding to use a self-help law book and to do your own legal work, you must realize that you are making a cost/value analysis and deciding that the chance your case will not turn out to your satisfaction is outweighed by the money you will save in doing it yourself. Most people handling their own simple legal matters never have a problem, but occasionally people find that it ended up costing them more to have an attorney straighten out the situation than it would have if they had hired an attorney in the beginning. Keep this in mind while handling your case, and be sure to consult an attorney if you feel you might need further guidance.

INTRODUCTION

Dividing property in the event of death or divorce can be a big headache, and can cost a small fortune in legal fees if a battle develops. If you have children from a previous marriage, the divorce laws of your state may deny them the share of your property you would like them to have. The probate laws may deny them everything in the event of your death. If you are getting married late in life, and have built up a successful business, the divorce or probate laws of your state may give a large share of your business to your spouse (or even force the sale of the business), even if the marriage was only for a short time. If your fiancé is wealthy, he or she (or his or her family) may be questioning your true intentions. These and many other problems connected with marriage can be solved by a contract known as a premarital agreement.

Even if you are already married, it is possible to enter into the same type of agreement with your spouse. In such a case it is called a *post-marital* agreement, but almost everything else will be similar. This book will use the word *premarital*, but you can just substitute *post-marital* if that is your situation.

This book will explain what a premarital agreement is, help you decide if you need one, and show you how to prepare one. By preparing your own agreement you can save the cost of a lawyer. And even if you decide to have a lawyer prepare an agreement for you, this book will help you to understand premarital agreements and work more effectively with your attorney.

This is not a law school course, but a practical guide to enable you to draft a legal contract without a lawyer. Legal jargon has been kept to a minimum. The emphasis is on practical advice in plain English. The terms *fiancé* and *fianceé* are used interchangeably.

Chapters 1 through 5 will give you information you need to understand premarital agreements. Chapter 6 will give you detailed instructions for preparing your own premarital agreement. Chapter 7 will tell you how to change or cancel your premarital agreement. Appendix A is a glossary of terms that you may see or hear in connection with premarital agreements. Appendix B gives information about the law relating to premarital agreements in each state. Appendix C contains the Uniform Premarital Agreement Act, which has been adopted by several states. Appendix D will give you some premarital agreement forms to use as models for preparing your premarital agreement.

WHAT IS A PREMARITAL AGREEMENT?

1

A premarital agreement is a contract between two persons planning to marry which determines the rights they have in each other's property. You may also see them called *antenuptial* agreements, or *prenuptial* agreements. Premarital agreements are used to control how property will be divided in the event of divorce or the death of one of the spouses. Some people even include non-financial rights and responsibilities, right down to who takes out the garbage and who does the dishes. However, since these types of agreements will not be enforced by the courts, they are better left out of the premarital agreement. If desired, these types of provisions should be part of a separate agreement that is just used to remind the husband and wife when problems arise.

Marriage contracts are nothing new. For hundreds, or even thousands, of years marriages have been based upon agreements between families and nations. Marriages were arranged by the parents in order to enhance family fortunes and to keep the peace between families and countries.

Most people don't fully appreciate the legal rights and obligations that are created when they marry. The legal aspects are often overlooked until it comes time for divorce. Then they find out that marriage is easy to get into, but difficult to get out of. The death of a spouse can also cause various problems with the couple's property.

When you get married, the law gives you and your spouse certain rights in each other's property. This includes property you acquire during your marriage, and may include property you acquired before you got married. The law also has provisions for how this property is handled in the event of divorce or death.

A premarital agreement might be considered a will for the death of a marriage (either due to actual death or to divorce). Just as a will can be used to avoid some of the hassles of probate, a premarital agreement can be used to avoid some of the hassles of divorce (and probate). Actually, everyone already has a will and a premarital agreement. These are called probate and divorce laws, which can be viewed as the will and premarital agreement the state writes for you if you don't write your own. The divorce laws and the probate laws of your state give guidelines for the judge to follow in determining how property should be divided or distributed. By using a premarital agreement you and your spouse can write your own guidelines to be used instead of your state's laws.

For a long time many courts would not enforce premarital agreements. The law has traditionally favored marriage. In the minds of law makers and judges, a premarital agreement seemed to encourage divorce, so the law makers would not approve them and the judges would not enforce them. But in more modern times, with *no-fault* divorce and the resulting high divorce rate, lawmakers and judges finally came to accept reality. Now, every state's laws allow for premarital agreements.

Let's take a look at how the divorce and probate laws generally affect a couple's property, and how a premarital agreement may help in each situation.

DIVORCE SITUATIONS

When a couple gets divorced they are required to divide up their property. If they cannot reach an agreement, the judge must decide who gets what. All states have guidelines which the judge must apply in making this decision. Although the exact wording is different in each state, the general ideas are the same and the following factors are typically considered:

1. Whether the property belonged to one of the spouses before they were married.

2. Whether the property acquired during the marriage was a gift to one spouse.

3. Whether the property was inherited by one spouse during the marriage.

4. Whether the property was acquired by exchanging one of the types of property mentioned above.

5. The length of the parties' marriage.

6. Each party's age and health.

7. Each party's financial circumstances, such as income, occupation, education and training, and employability.

8. Each party's contribution to the acquisition, preservation, or appreciation of property.

EXAMPLE   Let's look at one example of the type of problem that may occur in the event of a divorce. Joe and Maggie decide to get married. Both of them are thirty-eight years of age. Joe opened his own business a year ago and is still struggling to see his first profit. Maggie has no interest in helping Joe in his business. Maggie has a home, with a mortgage that will be paid off in six years, although it's a real struggle for her to keep up the payments and make necessary repairs. She is depending on having the house paid off as part of her retirement nest egg. They get married, and pool their money for their living expenses, including the mortgage payments and house repairs. Joe also does some repair and improvement work on the house. Joe continues with his business.

Three years later they decide to divorce. According to the divorce laws of their state, Maggie can claim part of Joe's business, and Joe can claim part of Maggie's house. If Joe's business is highly successful, he may have to borrow money to pay off Maggie's interest. This may get him in debt over his head and cause him to lose his business. Or he may have to sell the business to settle the divorce case. On the other hand, Maggie may need to refinance the house if she wants to buy out Joe's interest and keep her home. She may not be able to handle the new payments, and therefore, may have to sell the house. Even if she can make the new payments, it will take much more than six years to pay off the mortgage, which will destroy her retirement plans.

A premarital agreement could have avoided such problems. Joe has a potentially profitable business, but Maggie has no interest in his business and there is no assurance that it will become profitable. Maggie has some degree of security in her home, and Joe would have no interest in her home if they were not married. A premarital agreement could be written whereby Maggie would give up all rights to Joe's business in the event of divorce, and Joe would give up all rights to Maggie's home. This would preserve Maggie's retirement security, and would preserve for Joe the fruits of his labor in his business.

PROBATE SITUATIONS

When one spouse dies, either the state's probate laws or the person's will determines how property is distributed. This generally depends upon how the property was titled. Property may be titled, or *held*, in one of four ways:

1. **Sole ownership.** This is where all of the piece of property is titled to one person.

2. **Tenants in common.** This is where two or more people hold title together. If one of owners dies his or her share of the

property goes to his or her beneficiaries (by state law or will), and not automatically to the other owners.

3. **Joint tenants.** This is also where two or more people hold title together. However, if one owner dies his or her share automatically goes to the other owners. To make certain there is no room for debate, you will often see this stated as "joint tenants with rights of survivorship."

4. **Tenants by the entirety.** This is basically the same as joint tenants, except that it can only exist between a husband and wife. Tenancy by the entirety is not available in all states. In states that do not have this type of tenancy, it is typical for spouses to hold property as joint tenants.

Property held in both spouses' names (either as tenants by the entirety, or joint tenants) automatically becomes the sole property of the surviving spouse. What happens to other property (held by one spouse alone, or by both as tenants in common) depends upon whether there was a will.

If there was no will, the other property will generally go to the surviving spouse, unless there are children. Then it is typical for a portion to be given to the spouse, and a portion to be given to the children.

If there is a will, the other property will be distributed as directed in the will. However, most states make it impossible to deny property to the surviving spouse. In most states the surviving spouse is entitled to a certain share of the property, regardless of what the will says. This is called the surviving spouse's *elective share* or *forced share*.

EXAMPLE   Let's look at another example. Frank is divorced and has a son from his first marriage. Frank and Lois have been married for one year, and they do not have any children together. Lois is financially independent, as she has a large trust fund set up by her wealthy parents. Frank dies, leaving a will which leaves $10,000 to Lois, and the balance of his estate (his business which is worth $800,000) to his son who helped him for

9

fifteen years in his business. Under the laws of their state, Lois can claim one-half of Frank's estate, or $405,000. The main asset in Frank's estate is his business. This leaves Frank's son with a sad choice: either borrow $405,000 to pay off Lois' claim, take on Lois as a business partner, or sell the business to pay off Lois' claim. This is certainly not the situation Frank desired, and it could have been avoided with a premarital agreement.

These are only two examples of numerous situations where a premarital agreement could be of help. The next chapter will discuss this more, and help you decide if you can benefit from a premarital agreement.

DO YOU NEED A PREMARITAL AGREEMENT?

2

Your state government has created a plan for how your property will be divided in the event of divorce or death. The main question is: Are you are satisfied with the state's plan, or do you want your own plan? To answer this question, think about all of the ridiculous laws your state legislature has passed and how complicated they have made the laws, then ask yourself if you would trust any plan the legislature came up with on any subject.

Most state laws regarding the distribution of property after death or in the event of divorce leave plenty of room for a judge to "interpret." Therefore, one can never be sure what a judge will decide is really his or her property after a marriage. The only way to possibly avoid this is with a premarital agreement.

The question of whether you need a premarital agreement is difficult to answer. Many times the need does not become apparent until there is a divorce or a death. Then problems you never thought of tend to emerge. Anyone about to get married who thinks that divorce can never happen is not living in the real world. It is strange how the person who will buy a lottery ticket with odds of winning of only one in fifteen million, will refuse to recognize the chance of divorce in today's world. And some statistics suggest the divorce rate is higher in second marriages than in first marriages.

Also, don't forget that premarital agreements can be useful in the event of death, which is a subject even fewer of us seem comfortable thinking about. It's always strange to hear insurance salesmen talking about "in the event of death," as if some of us escape it altogether. Remember the old saying about life: "We're all in this together, and nobody gets out alive."

Most people think that a premarital agreement is what a rich person tries to get his or her non-rich fianceé to sign, in order to protect the rich person's property. Actually, there are many more reasons for a premarital agreement.

Let's examine a few common situations where a premarital agreement would be helpful.

First Marriages

Even if you and your partner are a young couple, with no significant property, typical jobs, and this is the first marriage for both of you, there is some evidence to indicate that premarital agreements actually promote stability in a marriage. This is because preparing one gives you a chance to think carefully about the significance of marriage, to clearly understand each other's financial situation, and to consider how you see your financial futures (individually and together). Discussing a premarital agreement, even if one is never finalized, will make you realize that, by getting married, you are entering into a legally binding contract, with financial rights and obligations. Usually this side of marriage is totally overshadowed by the romantic and religious aspects, and by the ceremony and honeymoon planning.

It is widely known that many married women do not know any of the details of their husband's finances. With so many women in the workforce today, and with many couples keeping separate bank accounts, many married men probably don't know the details of their wife's finances. Since one of the requirements of a premarital agreement is *full disclosure*, preparing one will help the couple get a clearer understanding of their total financial health. This can be very helpful in making financial decisions. If more couples had worked together on such things as purchasing decisions and monthly budgeting, perhaps the bankruptcy and divorce courts would not be as crowded as they are today.

It is also good for a couple to share common dreams and goals. While opposites may attract, such relationships do not tend to last. Focusing on a premarital agreement can bring the couple to discuss their career and economic goals in life. Especially with the common two-career couple, it is important to share thoughts on where each person intends his or her career to head. If each person is intent on developing his or her career, might it be a good idea for them to sign a premarital agreement giving up rights in each other's income or business? Especially if each has a fairly equivalent earning potential and they are just starting out in their careers? On the other hand, if they are in business together, a premarital agreement could outline how the business will be divided in the event of divorce. This would avoid large attorney fees later, if they instead fought over the business in a divorce proceeding.

CHILDREN OF PRIOR MARRIAGES

One of the main reasons for a premarital agreement is if one or both of the parties have children from a prior marriage. In such cases a premarital agreement may be the only way to assure that such children are protected in the event of divorce or death. Otherwise, all of your property may go to your second spouse, with your children getting nothing!

EXAMPLE   For example, suppose Rob and Rita are married and have no children together. Rob has two adult children from his former marriage. Rob dies without leaving a will. Under the laws of their state, all of Rob's property goes to Rita. Rob's children receive nothing.

A premarital agreement can help assure that children from a prior marriage will be provided for as intended by their parent. Your partner certainly should have no objection to you wanting to take care of your children. If your partner does object, it may be a good idea to reconsider your plans to marry.

BUSINESS OR INVESTMENT PARTNERS

If you have business partners, especially if they are family members, you should have a premarital agreement to prevent disruption of the business in the event of divorce or death. Otherwise, your partners (and even you) may end up with your spouse as a partner, and that can cause all kinds of problems.

This also applies if the business is a privately held corporation. Many problems have occurred when a spouse inherits stock, or receives stock as part of a divorce judgment.

EXAMPLE

For example, Mark and his brother Jim each hold fifty percent of the stock in a small restaurant business started by their father. Mark marries Jane, and several years later Mark dies, leaving Jane his half of the stock. Jane is now the partner of her brother-in-law Jim. Jane then marries Fred. When she and Fred divorce two years later, she gives Fred the stock in the restaurant as part of the property settlement. Now Jim has Fred for a partner. Is this what Mark would have wanted? Is this what Mark and Jim's father intended to happen to his family business?

Suppose Mark and Jane had divorced. A judge might divide the stock between them. Now Jim would have fifty percent, and Mark and Jane would have twenty-five percent each. Now Mark has his ex-wife as a business partner! Mark and Jim together could out-vote Jane, but what might happen if the relationship between Mark and Jim was strained to begin with? Now Jim and Jane might join forces to out-vote Mark.

WHAT ABOUT YOUR SITUATION ?

We have talked about divorce laws. Most states first divide property into two categories: marital property and nonmarital property. Generally, nonmarital property includes what each of you had before your marriage. If you are like most people, in the event you split up you would both want to keep what was yours before you got together. This sometimes becomes a problem if you can't prove what was yours before. In a premarital agreement you can write down what these nonmarital items are for each of you. That way there is no arguing later.

We have also talked about probate and wills. You may have family heirlooms, or other special items, that you would like to stay in your family.

EXAMPLE — For example, Diane has a diamond pendant that belonged to her great-grandmother. In the event of her death, Diane would want it to go to her sister. However, if she died without a will, the pendant will go to her husband. Even if she left the pendant to her sister in a will, her husband might have the right to the pendant if it is so valuable that it is a substantial portion of Diane's estate. Diane's husband might then marry, have a daughter by his new wife, and give the pendant to his daughter.

This type of situation is common in countless families, quite possibly including yours. In such cases, a premarital agreement might avoid undesirable results. You should consider a premarital agreement if any of the following situations apply:

1. You and your fiancé want to review your financial situation and plans for the future.

2. One or both of you have a business.

3. One or both of you are starting out on a career, or in a business, with potential for substantial financial growth.

4. One or both of you have significant property (including cash) that you want to preserve for yourself in the event of divorce.

5. One or both of you have certain items you want to preserve for someone else (such as a family member) in the event of divorce or death.

In addition to these situations, you need to examine your financial circumstances (including future plans for your career, business, or investments) and think about how they will be affected by a divorce or death.

Should You Hire a Lawyer? 3

Whether you need an attorney will depend upon several factors, such as how comfortable you feel handling the matter yourself, whether your financial situation is extremely complicated, and whether you have a very large estate to protect. If a lot of money is involved, you can, and should, hire a lawyer. As you will see in the next chapter, if your fiancé will be giving up a substantial amount it may be best if he or she sees a lawyer before signing anything.

One of the first questions you will want to consider, and most likely the reason you are reading this book, is: How much will an attorney cost? Attorneys come in all ages, shapes, sizes, sexes, racial and ethnic groups—and price ranges. Fees also will depend on how complicated your premarital agreement needs to be.

Selecting an attorney is not easy. It is difficult to know whether you are selecting an attorney you will be happy with. Most have probably never prepared a premarital agreement!

Selecting a Lawyer

Selecting a lawyer is a two-step process. First you need to decide which attorney to make an appointment with, then you need to decide if you want to hire that attorney.

FINDING
LAWYERS

The following suggestions will help you identify a few lawyers you may want to consider hiring:

- **Ask a friend.** A common, and frequently the best, way to find a lawyer is to ask someone you know to recommend one. This is especially helpful if the lawyer prepared a premarital agreement for your friend, or represented your friend in some other family law or probate matter.

- **Lawyer referral service.** You can find one by looking in the yellow pages phone directory under "Attorney Referral Services" or "Attorneys." This is a service, usually operated by a bar association, which is designed to match a client with an attorney handling cases in the area of law the client needs. A bar association referral service does not guarantee the quality of work, the level of experience, or the ability of the attorney. Some private referral services may offer some additional protections or guarantees. Finding a lawyer this way will at least connect you with one who is interested in family law matters, and probably has some experience in this area.

- **Yellow pages.** Check under the heading for "Attorneys" in the yellow pages phone directory. Many lawyers and law firms will place display ads here indicating their areas of practice and educational backgrounds. Look for firms or lawyers which indicate they practice in areas such as "divorce," "family law," "domestic relations," "probate," or "estate planning."

- **Ask a lawyer.** If you have used the services of an attorney in the past for some other matter (for example, a real estate closing, traffic ticket, or a will), you may want to call and ask if he or she handles premarital agreements, or could refer you to an attorney whose ability in this area is respected.

EVALUATING
LAWYERS

From your search you should select three to five lawyers worthy of further consideration. Your first step will be to call each attorney's office, explain that you are interested in having a premarital agreement prepared, and ask the following questions:

☛ Does the attorney (or firm) handle premarital agreements?

☛ How much can you expect it to cost?

☛ How soon can you get an appointment?

If you like the answers you get, ask if you can speak to the attorney. Some offices will permit this, but others will require you to make an appointment. Make the appointment if that is what is required. Once you get in contact with the attorney (either on the phone or at the appointment), ask the following questions:

☛ How much will it cost?

☛ How long has the attorney been in practice?

☛ How long has the attorney been in practice in your state?

☛ Has the attorney prepared premarital agreements before?

☛ How long will it take?

If you get acceptable answers to these questions, it's time to ask yourself the following questions about the lawyer:

☛ Do you feel comfortable talking to the lawyer?

☛ Is the lawyer friendly toward you?

☛ Does the lawyer seem confident in himself or herself?

☛ Does the lawyer seem to be straight-forward with you, and able to explain things so you understand?

If you get satisfactory answers to all of these questions, and feel comfortable with the lawyer, you probably have a lawyer you'll be able to work with.

WORKING WITH A LAWYER

In general, you will work best with your attorney if you keep an open, honest, and friendly attitude. You should also consider the following suggestions.

Clearly agree on what is to be done. Most attorneys ask for money "up front." You need your attorney to clearly tell you what will be done for this fee. Horror stories abound of attorneys using up $500 or $1,000 with nothing to show for it. Be sure that you are going to get a premarital agreement prepared in a form ready to be signed.

Ask questions. If you want to know something or if you don't understand something, ask your attorney. If you don't understand the answer, tell your attorney and ask him or her to explain it again. There are many points of law that many lawyers don't fully understand, so you should not be embarrassed to ask questions. Many people who say they had a bad experience with a lawyer either didn't ask enough questions, or had a lawyer who wouldn't take the time to explain things to them. If your lawyer isn't taking the time to explain what he's doing, it may be time to look for a new lawyer.

Give your lawyer complete information. Anything you tell your attorney is confidential. An attorney can lose his license to practice if he reveals information without your permission. So don't hold back. However, one of the basic principals of premarital agreements is "full disclosure." This means you will need to tell your fiancé about all of your property. If you hide anything it can be grounds for a court to refuse to enforce the premarital agreement!

Accept reality. Listen to what your lawyer tells you about the law, and accept it. It will do you no good to argue because the law doesn't work the way you think it should. By refusing to accept reality, you are only setting yourself up for disappointment. And remember: It's not your attorney's fault that the system isn't perfect, or that the law doesn't say what you'd like it to say.

Be patient. Don't expect your lawyer to return your phone call within an hour. He may not be able to return it the same day either. Most lawyers are very busy and over-worked. It is rare that an attorney can maintain a full caseload and still make each client feel as if he is the only client.

Talk to the secretary. Your lawyer's secretary can be a valuable source of information. So be friendly and get to know him or her. Often the secretary will be able to answer your questions, and you won't get a bill for the time you talk to the secretary.

Keeping things moving. Many lawyers operate on the old principle of "the squeaking wheel gets the oil." Work on a matter tends to get put off until a deadline is near, an emergency develops, or the client calls. This is because many lawyers take more cases than can be effectively handled in order to make the income they desire. Your task is to become a squeaking wheel that doesn't squeak so much that your attorney and his or her staff want to avoid you. Whenever you talk to your lawyer ask the following questions:

- ☞ What is the next step?
- ☞ When do you expect it to be done?
- ☞ When should I talk to you next?

If you don't hear from the lawyer when you expect, call him the following day. Don't remind him that he didn't call; just ask how things are going.

How to save money. Of course you don't want to spend unnecessary money for an attorney. Here are a few things you can do to avoid excess legal fees:

- ☞ Don't make unnecessary phone calls to your lawyer.
- ☞ Give information to the secretary whenever possible.

☞ Direct your question to the secretary first. Your question will be referred to the attorney if necessary.

☞ Plan your phone calls so you can get to the point and take less of your attorney's time. Make notes or an outline if necessary.

☞ Do some of the "leg work" yourself. Pick up and deliver papers yourself, for example. Ask your attorney what you can do to assist him or her.

☞ Be prepared for appointments. Have all related papers with you, plan your visit to get to the point, make an outline of what you want to discuss and what questions you want to ask.

Pay your attorney bill when it's due. No client gets prompt attention like a client who pays his lawyer on time. Many attorneys will have you sign an agreement which states how you will be charged.

Firing your lawyer. If you find that you can no longer work with your lawyer, or don't trust your lawyer, it is time to either go it alone or get a new attorney. You will need to send your lawyer a letter stating that you no longer desire his services, and are discharging him from representing you. Also state that you will be coming by his office the following day to pick up your file. The attorney does not have to give you his own notes or other work he has in progress, but he must give you the essential contents of your file (such as copies of papers already prepared and billed for, and any documents you provided). If he refuses to give you your file for any reason, contact your state's bar association about filing a complaint or *grievance*, against the lawyer. Of course, you will need to settle any remaining fees owed.

THE LAW OF 4
PREMARITAL
AGREEMENTS

IN GENERAL

The purpose of a carefully prepared premarital agreement is to make it legally binding and enforceable. If a court won't enforce a premarital agreement, it isn't worth the paper on which it is printed. This section will explain how courts look at premarital agreements, and how premarital agreements relate to divorce and probate law.

A BRIEF HISTORY

The law of premarital agreements has evolved over time. Originally, they were not recognized by some courts, because it was felt that premarital agreements somehow encouraged divorce. Eventually, they were enforced by courts, and the law regarding premarital agreements was slowly created in the opinions of the appellate courts. Next, state legislatures became involved, and premarital agreements were officially made a part of probate laws. These laws did not specifically apply to divorce situations, but the divorce courts began unofficially using them anyway. Finally, an independent "Uniform Premarital Agreement Act" was created which has been adopted in the following nineteen states: Arizona, Arkansas, California, Colorado, Hawaii, Illinois, Iowa, Kansas, Maine, Montana, Nevada, New Jersey, North Carolina, North Dakota, Oregon, Rhode Island, South Dakota, Texas, and Virginia.

UNIFORM PROBATE CODE PROVISION

A typical probate law provision is found in the "Uniform Probate Code," which has been adopted in many states, such as the following example from Alaska:

> **Sec. 13.11.085. Waiver of right to elect and of other rights.** The right of election of a surviving spouse and the rights of the surviving spouse to homestead allowance, exempt property and family allowance, or any of them, may be waived, wholly or partially, before or after marriage, by a written contract, agreement or waiver signed by the party waiving after full disclosure. Unless it provides to the contrary, a waiver of "all rights" (or equivalent language) in the property or estate of a present or prospective spouse or a complete property settlement entered into after or in anticipation of separation or divorce is a waiver of all rights to elective share, homestead allowance, exempt property and family allowance by each spouse in the property of the other and a renunciation by each of all benefits which would otherwise pass to that spouse from the other by intestate succession or by virtue of the provisions of any will executed before the waiver or property settlement.

THE COURTS AND PREMARITAL AGREEMENTS

Unfortunately, there is no absolute guarantee that a particular agreement will be enforced. Judge's do what they wish, and there is no way to predict what a particular judge will do in a particular case. All we can do is look at various decisions made by various courts, and try to avoid the pitfalls that defeated such agreements in the past. Ultimately, however, the judge will probably rule according to how he or she feels about the parties and the agreement they made. If the judge feels that both parties knew what they were doing, and the agreement is fair, the agreement will be enforced. If the judge feels that one party took unfair advantage of the other, the agreement will be declared invalid.

TYPES OF PREMARITAL AGREEMENTS

How a court looks at a premarital agreement may depend upon the husband's and wife's situations, and the type of premarital agreement. Premarital agreements may be divided, or broken down, into three types of provisions:

1. Those concerning the division of property upon the death of one party.

2. Those which simply set aside each party's separate property being brought into the marriage (in the event of divorce).

3. Those which concern rights in property acquired during the marriage (in the event of divorce).

Any premarital agreement may contain one or more of these types of provisions.

GUIDELINES To get an idea of how courts may look at a premarital agreement, it may be helpful to examine a particular case as an example. A good case for this is *Del Vecchio v. Del Vecchio,* 143 So.2d 17 (Florida Supreme Court 1962). The premarital agreement in this case gave a disproportionately small amount to the wife, especially considering the substantial property and income of the husband. The husband did not make full disclosure of his financial situation to the wife, although she did know that he had substantial business and property interests. The wife also did not have the advice of independent legal counsel before she signed the agreement.

The Florida Supreme Court did not address the particular agreement, but sent the case back to the trial court with instructions for the trial court to review the case again considering the following criteria:

1. Does the agreement make fair and reasonable provisions for the wife? (This could also be the husband if the wife is the person with the greater financial resources and the husband is giving up significant rights.) If it is fair and reasonable, then the agreement is valid. Whether the agreement is fair and reasonable should be determined by looking at the parties' relative situations, such as their ages, health, experience in financial matters, property held by each, and the needs of the wife (or husband). One question to be asked is: Whether, after a divorce, the wife (or husband) would be able to live in a

similar manner to that which he or she enjoyed before the marriage? The person must be able to live "certainly no less comfortably than before the marriage." The question of whether the agreement is fair and reasonable is determined with reference to the time at which the agreement was signed.

2. If the agreement is not fair and reasonable, then the court should ask: Was there full disclosure of husband's (or wife's) financial situation, and did the wife (or husband) have an understanding of her or his rights? If there was full disclosure and an understanding of rights, the agreement is valid.

3. If the agreement was not fair and reasonable, and there was not full disclosure, then the court should ask: Did the wife (or husband) have actual knowledge of, or should she or he have had a general knowledge of, the husband's (or wife's) property. If he or she had, or should have had, such knowledge, the agreement should probably be declared valid.

In considering the questions in items (2) and (3), the court will also look at whether the wife (or husband) had competent and independent legal advice, although such advice is not absolutely necessary to declare the agreement valid. Although the *Del Vecchio* case involved a probate situation, later cases followed it in divorce situations as well.

The *Del Vecchio* case is an example of how the Florida courts look at premarital agreements, but the same or similar factors are used in most states. The following things may also be considered, or have some bearing on whether a particular agreement will be declared valid.

Some courts have become ridiculous about having legal counsel. In the case of *In re Marriage of Kesler*, 4 Fam. L. Rptr. 2498 (Ohio Common Pleas 1978), the wife voluntarily chose not to have independent legal counsel advise her about the premarital agreement. The Ohio Court of Common Pleas decided that her choice was irrelevant, that she must have legal counsel even if she did not want it (due to the size and complexity of the husband's estate), and that the premarital agreement was therefore invalid. Here a woman signs a premarital agreement after declining legal advice, then uses her own voluntary action to have the agreement set aside. This is a perfect example of how unpredictable and irrational courts can be.

THE PARTIES

Where both parties have a similar value of property, and are fairly equal in their knowledge or experience about financial matters, the courts are likely to enforce the agreement. However, where one party has much more property or income than the other, or is much more financially sophisticated, the court will look more closely at such things as:

- ☛ Did the party with the advantage fully disclose the extent of his or her property and income to the other party?

- ☛ Are the provisions of the agreement fair and reasonable to the other party?

- ☛ Did the other party freely and voluntarily sign the agreement?

- ☛ Did the other party have the advice of independent legal counsel before signing the agreement?

DIVISION UPON DEATH PROVISIONS

These provisions relate to probate laws. Although the details of probate law vary from state to state, there are some general principles which apply in most, if not all, states. Upon the death of a spouse, the distribution of property depends upon whether there is a will. If there is not a will, the state laws will determine who gets the property. These laws assure that the surviving spouse receives a certain portion of the property. If there are no children, the spouse usually gets it all. If there are children, the property usually gets apportioned between the spouse and the children. The surviving spouse may get a set percentage of the estate, or may have the right to live in the marital home until death. This right may only apply to the wife in some states.

If there is a will, it decides who gets the property. However, state laws still assure the surviving spouse (again possibly only the wife) a minimal amount of the estate.

EXAMPLE   For example, suppose that Jack dies. His will leaves $1,000 to his wife Jill, and leaves the rest of his property (valued at $299,000) to The Wishing Well Foundation, Jack's favorite charity. Jill can take advantage of her state's law regarding a spouse's elective share, and get one-third of Jack's estate (or $100,000). The amount of the elective share varies from state to state, but the principle is the same.

By signing a premarital agreement, a spouse can give up such rights to minimal amounts of his or her spouse's estate. In such cases the judge will want to be sure that the surviving spouse will not be left destitute, that he or she knew the extent of the other's estate when the agreement was signed, and knew what rights were being given up.

SEPARATE PROPERTY

Traditionally, courts would not enforce premarital agreements dealing with divorce. Such agreements were considered to encourage divorce, and the government wanted to encourage marriage. Now that divorce is much more common, the courts and the legislatures have come around to face reality, and premarital agreements are more acceptable.

Most, if not all, states recognize the concept of *separate property* in a marriage. You may also see separate property referred to as *nonmarital property* or *sole property*. Generally, in a divorce all property acquired during the marriage is considered *marital* property. In some states it is called *community* property. (There are legal technical differences between marital and community property, but for purposes of our discussion here these differences are not important.) Marital property is jointly owned by the parties, and will be fairly equally divided between them in a divorce. Typical examples of separate property are:

☞ Property owned by one party before the marriage.

☞ Property acquired during the marriage, but as a gift to one party individually.

☞ Property acquired during the marriage, but as an inheritance by one party individually.

☞ Any property acquired during the marriage by exchanging any of the types of property described above.

The listing for your state in appendix B of this book will give you an idea of how your state laws view separate property.

Since the idea of separate property is so widely recognized and used, the courts will usually enforce a premarital agreement or provision which simply designates what property is separate. This is the type of provision which is the most likely to be enforced in court.

Property Acquired During Marriage

Premarital agreements dealing with how property acquired during the marriage will be distributed upon divorce or death will be more carefully reviewed by courts. Generally, property acquired during the marriage is considered joint property (or community property), regardless of how the title is held. The standard provision in a premarital agreement is to reverse this, and make how title is held the determining factor as to whether the property is joint or separate. This allows the couple to determine how each piece of property is held, as they acquire it. For example, if they want it to be solely owned by the wife, only her name would appear on the title. Wherever title is unclear, the court will probably determine the property to be joint or community property.

CIRCUMSTANCES WHEN SIGNED

The court may also look at the circumstances that existed at the time the premarital agreement was signed. Was one party under any kind of pressure to sign the agreement? If the person was threatened, pressured, coerced, or unduly influenced to sign the agreement, the court will declare the agreement invalid. Another question is whether the person had sufficient time to consider what he or she was about to sign. Do not have the agreement signed only a few hours or minutes before the wedding. Each party should have a copy of the agreement for several days (a week or two would be even better) before signing it. This will allow enough time for the person to study it, think about it, and have it reviewed by independent legal and financial advisers, before signing. It should also be signed well before the day of the wedding. At least a week before would be advisable. Delaware law actually requires that it be signed at least ten days before the marriage.

ALIMONY, CHILD SUPPORT, AND CHILD CUSTODY

Provisions to eliminate or limit alimony will also be upheld where there was full disclosure. If both parties are in roughly equal financial situations, mutual waivers of alimony will be no problem. However, alimony provisions in premarital agreements are usually viewed in terms of the parties' situations at the time the agreement is signed. A later change in circumstances may cause problems with enforcing such provisions.

EXAMPLE   For example, suppose that Fred and Ginger are in fairly equal financial positions at the time they sign a premarital agreement mutually waiving alimony. Both have jobs earning about the same income, and they have property of approximately equal value. Five years later, Ginger is involved in a serious automobile accident which leaves her permanently disabled and unable to continue working. Should either of them file for divorce, the court is unlikely to uphold the alimony waiver provision of the premarital agreement. Similarly, courts will not enforce an alimony waiver or limitation which would leave one spouse without sufficient support, especially if that spouse would need government assistance.

Child support and custody provisions which are reasonable, and leave the child adequately cared for, will probably be upheld. However, most state divorce laws have criteria for determining custody, and a formula for determining child support. An agreement will not be upheld if it would not provide adequate child support (such as if it is substantially less than the state's child support formula), or has a custody arrangement that is clearly against the child's best interest (such as giving custody to a convicted child abuser).

PENSION PLANS

When it comes to divorce law, one of the most difficult assets to deal with is a pension or retirement plan. Generally, a pension plan is considered a marital asset to be divided between the parties. For some couples, this is one of the largest assets they have. If both parties are employed, and have pension plans of fairly equal value, they will probably each keep their own plan. In this situation a provision in a premarital agreement whereby both parties waive any interest in each other's plan will probably be upheld.

However, problems can arise where only one party has a pension plan, or where one party's plan is significantly more valuable than the other's. In these situations one party's plan will need to be evaluated by a professional to determine how much of it belongs to the other. This can be a complex calculation, taking into consideration such things as the length of marriage, the length of time the parties will probably work, the length of time the parties are likely to live beyond retirement, etc.

Still, if the party giving up these rights understands what is being given up, and does so voluntarily, the waiver will probably be upheld.

To further complicate things, the United States Circuit Court of Appeals for the Second Circuit recently ruled that pension rights could only be waived by a spouse, not by a fiancé. This means that you may need a post-marital agreement (instead of a premarital agreement) in order to effectively waive pension rights. Appropriate clauses for a premarital agreement and a post-marital agreement waiver of pension rights are included later in this book.

THE LAW IN YOUR STATE

To find out about the law for your state, you will first need to refer to the listing for your state in appendix B of this book, which will give you some basic information about the law in your state. More information about how to use appendix B is found in later chapters and at the beginning of appendix B. It is also strongly suggested that you visit a law library. The next section of this chapter will give you more information about using the law library.

LEGAL RESEARCH

In order to be certain that you are doing things correctly, you may need to do a little research into the law in your state. Appendix B of this book provides some information regarding the law in each state, and will give you a starting point for looking further.

After this book, you may want to visit your local law library. One can usually be found in, or near, your county courthouse. If you live near a law school, you can also find a library there. Don't hesitate to ask the law librarian to help you find what you need. The librarian cannot give you legal advice, but can show you where to find your state's laws and other books on premarital agreements. Some typical sources are discussed below.

STATUTES OR
CODES

The main source of information will be the set of volumes which contain the laws passed by your state legislature. Depending upon your state, these will be referred to as either the "statutes," or the "code" of your state. For example: "Florida Statutes," or "Mississippi Code." The actual title of the books may also include words such as "Revised," or "Annotated." For example: "Annotated California Code," "Illinois Statutes Annotated," "Kentucky Revised Statutes," or "Maine Revised Statutes Annotated." "Revised" simply means updated, and "annotated" means that the books contain summaries of court decisions and other information which explain and interpret the laws. In some states the titles will also include the name of the publisher, such as "*West's* Colorado Revised Statutes Annotated," "*Vernon's* Annotated Missouri Statutes," or "*Purdon's* Pennsylvania Consolidated Statutes Annotated." The listing for your state in appendix B gives the title of the set of laws for your state under the heading "THE LAW." A few states have more than one set of laws, by various publishers. For example: Florida has both "Florida Statutes" and "Florida Statutes Annotated." Michigan has both "Michigan Statutes Annotated" and "Michigan Compiled Laws Annotated." Each state's listing in appendix B will give the name of the set of books used by the author. Ask the law librarian for help if you have any problems in locating your state's laws.

Each year the legislature meets and changes the law, therefore, it is important to be sure you have the most current version. Once you locate the set of books at the library, you will find that they are updated in one of three ways. The most common way to update laws is with a soft-cover supplement, which will be found in the back of each volume. There will be a date on the cover of the supplement to tell you when it was published (such as "1998 Cumulative Supplement"). If it is more than one year old, ask the librarian if it is the most current supplement. Another way laws are updated is with a supplement volume, which will be found at the end of the regular set of volumes. This will also have a date or year on it. A few states use a looseleaf binding, in which pages are removed and replaced, or a supplement section added, as the law changes.

PRACTICE
MANUALS

At the law library, you may also be able to find practice manuals, which are books containing detailed information about various aspects of the law. You may find practice manuals about premarital agreement law in your state, including sample forms for all different situations. Some of these books are written in connection with seminars for lawyers and they can be very helpful in answering your questions about very specific situations. Again, ask the librarian to help you.

You probably won't need to do any more research than to look up any laws your state may have regarding premarital agreements, and look at some of the forms in a practice manual. However, just in case you need (or want) to go further with your research, the following information is provided. In addition to the laws passed by the legislature, law is also made by the decisions of the judges in various cases each year. To find this *case law* you will need to go to a law library. In addition to annotated codes or statutes, there are several types of books used to find the case law:

DIGESTS

A *digest* is a set of volumes which gives short summaries of appeals court cases, and tells you where you can find the court's full written opinion. The information in the digest is arranged alphabetically by subject. First, try to find a digest for your state (such as "New York Digest"). There is a digest which covers the entire United States, but it will be easier to find your state's laws in a state digest. Look for the chapter on "Premarital Agreements," "Antenuptial Agreements," or "Marriage," then look for the headings for the subject you want. If you can't find a chapter with one of these titles, look in the index under these words to find out what chapter title you should use.

CASE
REPORTERS

A case reporter is where the appeals courts publish their written opinions on the cases they hear. There may be a specific reporter for your state, or you may need to use a regional reporter which contains cases from several states in your area. Your librarian can help you locate the reporter for your state. There may be two *series* of the regional reporter, the second series being newer than the first. For example, if the digest gives a reference to "*Del Vecchio v. Del Vecchio,* 143 So.2d 17 (1962)," this tells you that you can find the case titled *Del Vecchio v. Del Vecchio* by going to Volume 143 of the *Southern Reporter 2d Series,* and turning to page 17. The number in parentheses (1962) is the year the court issued its opinion. In its opinion, the court will discuss what the case was about, what questions of law were presented for consideration, and what the court decided and why.

LEGAL ENCYCLOPEDIA

A legal encyclopedia is similar to a regular encyclopedia. You simply look up the subject you want (such as "Premarital Agreements," "Marriage," "Divorce," etc.), in alphabetical order, and it gives you a summary of the law on that subject. It will also refer to specific court cases, which can then be found in the Reporter. On a national level, the two main sets are *American Jurisprudence* (abbreviated "Am. Jur."), and *Corpus Juris Secundum* ("C.J.S."). You may also find a set for your state, such as *Florida Jurisprudence.*

Talking to Your Partner 5

There is no clear cut way to talk to all people about premarital agreements. Each person has a different experience, background and attitude about the subject, so the same approach will not work with everyone. All that can be done is to offer several suggestions and ideas, so that you can choose or design an approach that you think will be the best for your situation.

It is important for you to realize that discussion of a premarital agreement will probably contain both logical and emotional aspects. The emotional aspect will be more difficult to anticipate and deal with.

The idea of a premarital agreement is not popular with many people. The main reason for this is that it appears to be looking toward a divorce, even before the couple is married. This is similar to how many people don't make a will because it means they have to think about death. The world would probably be a much more pleasant place if we didn't have to deal with death, divorce, and taxes. Unfortunately, we don't have such luxury.

Many people also think that a premarital agreement diminishes the romance of marriage. In fact, the mention of a premarital agreement may be the easiest way to get an engagement broken! Therefore, it can be important to bring up the subject in the right way. This may depend upon the relative financial positions of you and your intended spouse.

If you are both of roughly equal wealth, you would approach the subject differently than if you are a wealthy person about to marry someone of average means. Let's examine some ideas that may be useful to you.

First of all, think about the central question: Why would someone want to sign a premarital agreement? The answer is: Because the agreement is fair, and I get some kind of protection or advantage from it. You cannot expect your partner to sign (or even be receptive to the idea) of a one-sided agreement.

To deal with the potential emotional reaction, you may want to begin with a general discussion of planning your financial future together. This is important for any individual or couple, even if they don't want a premarital agreement. Several years ago Harvard University conducted a study of its graduates. It found that three percent had specific written goals, ten percent had goals in mind but not written, and eighty-seven percent had not set goals. The three percent with specific written goals accomplished fifty to 100 times more in their lifetimes than the ten percent with goals in their mind only. Comparatively very little was accomplished by the ninety-seven percent with no *written* goals.

Therefore, it is important for the two of you to plan for your future. This will involve talking about your dreams and desires for your careers, for having children and for their future, and what kind of a lifestyle you want to seek. Part of financial planning includes examining your life insurance needs, and this may lead to a discussion of having wills prepared. As we've discussed earlier, in many situations a will may be insufficient to accomplish what is intended, and a premarital agreement can cure this problem.

The ideal way to prepare a premarital agreement is for the two of you to prepare it together. This way, it is not perceived that one of you is asking the other to sign one. In fact, Dale Carnegie, in his book *How To Win Friends and Influence People*, says the best way to win someone to your point of view is to make that person think it was his or her idea!

This might be done by describing a possible problem to your partner, and asking him or her how to resolve it. A little prompting might be necessary of course: "Do you think some kind of premarital agreement might take care of this?"

Another way to lead into this discussion might be something like: "I read somewhere that a premarital agreement is a good idea. I'm not sure what I think of the idea, do you think we should consider it?" Or: "My lawyer (or account, financial planner, estate planner, mother, business partner, etc.) suggested we should get wills and a premarital agreement prepared. What do you think about that?" Or: "Someone at work gave me this book to look at. I looked through it briefly, and it looks like a premarital agreement might be a good idea in addition to wills."

The other way is for you to prepare a premarital agreement, then present it to your partner for his or her consideration and comment. If you take this route, however, you should approach it with how it will protect or benefit your intended spouse. This might involve reminding him or her of problems with a previous marriage ("so you won't need to worry about that happening again"). You might also begin by explaining a problem you had with a previous marriage.

In any event, you will both need to believe the agreement is fair. If the agreement is not fair to your partner, don't expect him or her to sign it. If you truly feel it is fair, and your partner won't sign it, then maybe you should reconsider the marriage. Of course, be sure to listen to his or her objections, because you will want to be sure your proposal is fair. One final thought: If you and your partner can't discuss this, then maybe one or both of you are not ready (mature, honest, practical, or sufficiently able to communicate) for marriage.

PREPARING YOUR PREMARITAL AGREEMENT

6

Usually a premarital agreement must be somewhat tailored to your specific situation. This chapter will guide you in preparing your own agreement. First we will discuss the two premarital agreement forms in appendix D. The first is a basic agreement, designed for the situation where the two persons are in fairly simple and equal financial situations. The second form is for more complicated situations.

Next, we will discuss the various additional forms which you may need to attach to your agreement. These are:

- ☞ HUSBAND'S FINANCIAL STATEMENT (Form 3). This satisfies the husband's duty for full disclosure.

- ☞ WIFE'S FINANCIAL STATEMENT (Form 4). This satisfies the wife's duty for full disclosure.

- ☞ HUSBAND'S SCHEDULE OF SEPARATE PROPERTY (Form 5).

- ☞ WIFE'S SCHEDULE OF SEPARATE PROPERTY (Form 6).

- ☞ SCHEDULE OF JOINT PROPERTY (Form 7).

- ☞ EXPENSE PAYMENT SCHEDULE (Form 8). This describes how you and your partner will handle monthly living expenses.

- ☞ ADDENDUM TO PREMARITAL AGREEMENT (Form 9). This is used if you need more space.

BASIC PREMARITAL AGREEMENT (FORM 1)

The basic premarital agreement form (Form 1) is designed for a couple who are of fairly equal financial and career situations, and desire to keep most or all of their finances separate. With this form, each person gives up all interests in the other's property and earnings, unless they specifically indicate otherwise in writing (such as by purchasing property together and having it titled in both names).

As you will see, there are not many blank spaces that need to be filled in on this form. On the next two pages are the first and last pages of Form 1, shown completed for a fictional couple. There are two boxes at the bottom right-hand corner of each page. These are for you and your partner to initial to indicate that you have read and approve each page. Note that paragraph 29 allows for you to use the ADDENDUM TO PREMARITAL AGREEMENT (Form 9) for any additional provisions needed for your particular circumstances.

After you have completed your agreement, you will need to get two witnesses and go to a notary public for the signing. You, your fiancé, and your two witnesses will sign the agreement before the notary. The notary will complete the rest of the form. Your witnesses should not be anyone who would inherit from either of you, either by law or in your wills.

PREMARITAL AGREEMENT

This Agreement is entered into on ___August 23___, ___1998___, by and between ___Stanley I. Kowalski___ (hereafter referred to as the Husband), and ___Blanche E. DuBois___ (hereafter referred to as the Wife), who agree that:

1.   MARRIAGE. The parties plan to marry each other, and intend to provide in this agreement for their property and other rights that may arise because of their contemplated marriage.

2.   PURPOSE OF AGREEMENT. Both parties currently own assets, and anticipate acquiring additional assets, which they wish to continue to control and they are executing this Agreement to fix and determine their respective rights and duties during the marriage, in the event of a divorce or dissolution of the marriage, or on the death of one of the parties.

3.   FINANCIAL DISCLOSURE. The parties have fully revealed to each other full financial information regarding their net worth, assets, holdings, income, and liabilities; not only by their discussions with each other, but also through copies of their current financial statements, copies of which are attached hereto as Exhibit A and Exhibit B. Both parties acknowledge that they have had sufficient time to review the other's financial statement, are familiar with and understand the other's financial statement, have had any questions satisfactorily answered, and are satisfied that full and complete financial disclosure has been made by the other.

4.   ADVICE OF COUNSEL. Each party has had legal and financial advice, or has the opportunity to consult independent legal and financial counsel, prior to executing this agreement. Either party's failure to so consult legal and financial counsel constitutes a waiver of such right. By signing this agreement, each party acknowledges that he or she understands the facts of this agreement, and is aware of his or her legal rights and obligations under this agreement or arising because of their contemplated marriage.

5.   CONSIDERATION. The parties acknowledge that each of them would not enter into the contemplated marriage except for the execution of this agreement in its present form.

6.   EFFECTIVE DATE. This Agreement shall become effective and binding upon the marriage of the parties. In the event the marriage does not take place, this agreement shall be null and void.

7.   DEFINITIONS. As used in this agreement, the following terms shall have the following meanings:
        (a)   "Joint Property" means property held and owned by the parties together. Such ownership shall be as tenants by the entirety in jurisdictions where such a tenancy is permitted. If such jurisdiction does not recognize or permit a tenancy by the entirety, then ownership shall

SJK	BED

27.   PARAGRAPH HEADINGS. The headings of the paragraphs contained in this agreement are for convenience only, and are not to be considered a part of this agreement or used in determining its content or context.

28.   ATTORNEYS' FEES IN ENFORCEMENT. A party who fails to comply with any provision or obligation contained in this agreement shall pay the other party's attorneys' fees, costs, and other expenses reasonably incurred in enforcing this agreement and resulting from the non-compliance.

29.   SIGNATURES AND INITIALS OR PARTIES. The signatures of the parties on this document, and their initials on each page, indicate that each party has read, and agrees with, this entire Premarital Agreement, including any and all exhibits attached hereto. Any provisions containing a box, ❏, which does not contain an "X" does not apply and is not a part of the agreement of the parties.

30.   ❏   OTHER PROVISIONS. Additional provisions are contained in the Addendum to Premarital Agreement attached hereto and made a part hereof.

_*Stanley I Kowalski*_____
Husband

_*Blanche E. DuBois*_____
Wife

Executed in the presence of:

_*Ralph Kramden*_____
Name:_ Ralph Kramden _____
Address:_ 142 Tennessee Ave. _
_ Williams, VA _____

_*Alice Kramden*_____
Name:_ Alice Kramden _____
Address:_ 142 Tennessee Ave. _
_ Williams, VA _____

STATE OF   )
COUNTY OF   )

     The foregoing instrument was acknowledged before me this _____ day of _____, _____, by _ Stanley I. Kowalski, Blanche E. DuBois, Ralph Kramden, & Alice Kramden _

the above-named Husband, Wife and Witnesses respectively, who are personally known to me or who have produced _ VAdr.lic.K-492-729, D603-997,K559-382, K193-449 _ as identification.

_____
Signature

_ Trixie Norton _____
(Typed Name of Acknowledger)

NOTARY PUBLIC
Commission Number:_ 97-299384 _
My Commission Expires: Nov. 23, 2001

TAILORED PREMARITAL AGREEMENT (FORM 2)

If you determine that you are unable to use Form 1, you will need to create your own agreement using Form 2 as a guide. Form 2 may be used "as is," by checking the boxes which are appropriate to your situation; or you may want to write a new agreement only using the provisions you have selected or agreed upon. There are advantages and disadvantages to each method.

If you are trying to get your partner to agree to the provisions you want, you may not want him or her to see the alternatives. In this case it would be better to prepare an agreement containing only those provisions you want. On the other hand, if the other alternatives are in your agreement, it will show that the agreement was voluntarily signed and agreed to with knowledge of alternatives. This will help your position later, should your partner try to say that you talked him or her into signing, or that he or she didn't understand the options.

In the sample agreement on pages 49 through 58, the fictional couple has selected various optional provisions from Form 2 as found in appendix D, and has created their own agreement. The following instructions, referring to the numbered paragraphs in Form 2, will help you complete or use this form:

1. First, unnumbered paragraph: Type in the date, the husband's name, and wife's name where indicated. The date should be the same date as you will sign the agreement before the witnesses and the notary.

2. Paragraphs 1, 5 through 13, 16, 17, 22 through 26, and 28 through 35, can be left alone. Of course, they may need to be renumbered if you are creating your own agreement and leave one or more paragraphs out.

3. Paragraph 2: If you or your partner have children from a prior marriage, check both "A" and "B." Then check the appropriate

box or boxes to indicate whose children they are, and type in the names of the children on the line. If there are no such children, check "A" only.

4. Paragraph 3: Check whichever item is appropriate to your situation. It is preferable to check "A." Item "B" should only be used if one or both parties is not provided with the other's financial statement (this is more likely to prompt a court challenge to the agreement). Also, if item "B" is checked, the box for either "Husband" or "Wife" should be checked.

5. Paragraph 4: Check the appropriate box to reflect your situation. Only check one box. For items "A" and "B" the name of the person or persons giving counsel should be typed in on the appropriate lines. For item "B" either the box for "Husband" or "Wife" should be checked.

6. Paragraph 14: Check only one box, as appropriate for your situation. Item "A" is more restrictive in that it simply keeps everything related to separate property separate. Item "B" is more generous, and more in agreement with most state divorce laws.

7. Paragraph 15: Check only one box. Item "A" is the more restrictive of the two. Also check the box for "Husband" or "Wife."

8. Paragraph 18: Check only one box. Item "A" allows no alimony at all. Item "B" provides for a lump sum alimony based upon the number of years of marriage. Item "C" provides for temporary and rehabilitative alimony for a fixed period of time. Item "D" provides for permanent alimony. If item "B," "C," or "D" is checked, also check the box for either "Husband" or "Wife;" and type in the agreed upon amount after the $ symbol. For items "C" or "D" a period (such as "week" or "month") will need to be typed in after the word "per." In item "C" the number of years alimony is to be paid will need to be filled in after the words "period of."

9. Paragraph 19: This paragraph contains spaces for you and your partner to type in the percentage each of you would contribute toward child support needs for your children. It also contains three choices for how long child support would continue.

10. Paragraph 20: Check only one box as appropriate. Item "A" is more restrictive, providing that both parties give up all rights to inherit from the other, unless a provision is made in the person's will. Item "B" provides for a minimum inheritance, and as such is more likely to be enforced by a court. If item "B" is used, the boxes for either "Husband" or "Wife" will need to be checked, and an amount will need to be filled in after the $ symbol.

11. Paragraph 21: If no life insurance is to be required, type in "None" after the $ symbol. Otherwise, the agreed upon amount will need to be typed in.

12. Paragraph 27: Type in the name of the state whose law you wish to have applied to your agreement. This will usually be the state where you live, or where you intend to live after you are married.

13. Paragraph 36: Check this box if there are any additional provisions to your agreement. Such provisions will need to be typed in on the Addendum to Premarital Agreement (Form 9).

14. There is a box at the bottom right-hand corner of each page of the agreement. You should write your initials in one box on each page, and your partner should initial the other box. This indicates that you have read, and agree to, the provisions on each page.

15. You and your partner should go with your two witnesses to a notary for signing of the agreement. You and your partner will sign on the line above the words "Husband" and "Wife." The

witnesses will sign on the lines below the words "Executed in the presence of:", and their names and addresses should be typed below their signatures. The notary will complete the bottom portion of the form.

PREMARITAL AGREEMENT

This Agreement is entered into on ___March 23___, ___1998___, by and between ___George Washington___ (hereafter referred to as the Husband), and ___Martha Dandridge Curtis___ (hereafter referred to as the Wife), who agree that:

1. **MARRIAGE.**

   The parties plan to marry each other, and intend to provide in this agreement for their property and other rights that may arise because of their contemplated marriage.

2. **PURPOSE OF AGREEMENT.**

   (A) Both parties currently own assets, and anticipate acquiring additional assets, which they wish to continue to control, and are executing this Agreement to establish and determine their respective rights and responsibilities during the marriage, in the event of a divorce or dissolution of the marriage, or the death of one of the parties.

   (B) The parties desire that each party having any child(ren) of a prior marriage be able to identify and maintain a separate estate so as to provide for such child(ren), and each party has the following children of a prior marriage:

   ❑ Husband:_____.
   ☒ Wife:___John Parke Curtis_____.

3. **FINANCIAL DISCLOSURE.**

   The parties have fully revealed to each other complete financial information regarding their net worth, assets, holdings, income, and liabilities; both by their discussions with each other, and through their current financial statements, copies of which are attached hereto as Exhibits A and Exhibit B. Both parties acknowledge that they have had sufficient time to review the other's financial statement, are familiar with and understand the other's financial statement, have had any questions satisfactorily answered, and are satisfied that full and complete financial disclosure has been made by the other.

4. **ADVICE OF COUNSEL.**

   Each party has had advice of independent counsel prior to executing this agreement.

   The Husband received such counsel from ___John Jay, attorney at law___.
   The Wife received such counsel from ___Daniel Webster, attorney at law___.

   | GW | MDC |

As a result of such independent counsel, both parties acknowledge that they have been informed of their legal rights in the property currently owned by each of them, rights in any property which may be acquired by either or both of them during their marriage, rights to claim interests in such property, rights to seek alimony upon divorce or dissolution of marriage, rights of inheritance and support as a surviving spouse, rights to take a certain share of the other's estate in the event the other's will makes unacceptable provisions for him or her, and has been informed of the consequences of any waivers, releases and surrenders of such rights pursuant this agreement.

5.   **CONSIDERATION.**

The parties acknowledge that each of them would not enter into the contemplated marriage except for the execution of this agreement.

6.   **EFFECTIVE DATE.**

This Agreement shall become effective and binding upon the marriage of the parties. In the event the marriage does not take place, this agreement shall be null and void.

7.   **DEFINITIONS.**

As used in this agreement, the following terms shall have the following meanings:

(a) "Joint Property" means property held and owned by the parties together. Such ownership shall be as tenants by the entirety in jurisdictions where such a tenancy is permitted. If such jurisdiction does not recognize or permit a tenancy by the entirety, then ownership shall be as joint tenants with rights of survivorship. The intention of the parties is to hold joint property as tenants by the entirety whenever possible. "Joint property" also means community property as to any property which may be subject to community property laws.

(b) "Joint Tenancy" means tenancy by the entirety in jurisdictions where such a tenancy is permitted, and joint tenancy with rights of survivorship if tenancy by the entirety is not recognized or permitted. The intention of the parties is to hold joint property as tenants by the entirety whenever possible. "Joint tenancy" also refers to community property as to any property which may be subject to community property laws.

| *GW* | | *MDC* |

(c) "Separate Property" means property owned by either party which is and will remain, or may be acquired, as that party' individual property, free from any claims of the other party. "Separate property" is not part of the community property estate in any state recognizing community property.

8. **HUSBAND'S SEPARATE PROPERTY.**

The Husband is the owner of certain property, which is set forth and described in Exhibit C attached hereto and made a part hereof, which he intends to keep as his nonmarital, separate, sole, and individual property. All income, rents, profits, interest, dividends, stock splits, gains, and appreciation in value, relating to any such separate property shall also be deemed separate property. All inheritances or gifts received by the Husband individually during the marriage shall also be deemed separate property.

9. **WIFE'S SEPARATE PROPERTY.**

The Wife is the owner of certain property, which is set forth and described in Exhibit D attached hereto and made a part hereof, which she intends to keep as her nonmarital, separate, sole, and individual property. All income, rents, profits, interest, dividends, stock splits, gains, and appreciation in value, relating to any such separate property shall also be deemed separate property. All inheritances or gifts received by the Wife individually during the marriage shall also be deemed separate property.

10. **JOINT OR COMMUNITY PROPERTY.**

The parties intend that certain property shall, from the beginning of the marriage, be joint property, as set forth and described in Exhibit E attached hereto and made a part hereof.

11. **PROPERTY ACQUIRED DURING MARRIAGE.**

The parties recognize that either or both of them may acquire property during the marriage. The parties agree that the manner in which such property is titled during the marriage shall control such property's ownership and distribution in the event of divorce, dissolution of marriage, separation, or death of either party. Such property shall be held as stated in the instrument conveying or evidencing title . If the instrument does not specify or if there is no instrument, the property shall be held as a tenancy by the entirety, or as a joint tenancy with rights of survivorship in the event tenancy by the entirety is not recognized by the state having jurisdiction over the distribution of such property. Any property acquired

GW	MDC

that does not normally have a title or ownership certificate shall be considered as joint property unless otherwise specified by the parties in writing. All wedding gifts shall be deemed joint property, unless specified as separate property in either Exhibit C or D.

12. BANK ACCOUNTS.

Any funds deposited in either party's separate bank accounts shall be deemed that party's separate property. Any funds deposited in a bank account held by the parties jointly shall be deemed joint property.

13. PAYMENT OF EXPENSES.

The parties agree that their expenses shall be paid as set forth in Exhibit F attached hereto and made a part hereof.

14. INCOME FROM AND REINVESTMENT OF SEPARATE PROPERTY.

Any property obtained by either party due to the use, investment, reinvestment or any transfer of any portion of his or her separate property, and any income from any such property, shall remain that party's separate property. Any appreciation or other increase in the value of either party's separate property, shall remain that party's separate property, unless the other party has made a direct financial contribution to the increase in value, but only to the proportion of the increase attributable to his or her contribution.

15. RESIDENCE OF THE PARTIES.

It is expressly recognized that the ☒ Husband ☐ Wife is the sole owner of the residence to be occupied by the parties at ___123 Mt. Vernon Ave.___, and that the use of any joint funds, or separate funds of the other party, for the mortgage payments, utilities, repair or maintenance of the residence and grounds for the joint benefit of the parties shall not create any interest in the property in the other party. However, if joint funds or the other party's separate funds are used to make capital improvements on the property, the other party shall have a lien against the property to the extent of one-half of the total joint funds, or the full amount of the separate funds, contributed, which lien shall be paid upon the sale of the property, the termination of the marriage, or the death of the Husband or Wife, whichever occurs first.

| GW | MDC |

16. DISPOSITION OF PROPERTY.

Each party retains the ownership, management and control of his or her separate property, and may encumber, sell, or dispose of the property without the other party's consent. Each party shall, on the request of the other, execute any instrument necessary to effectuate this paragraph. The failure ore refusal of a party to join in or execute an instrument required by this paragraph shall entitle the other party to sue for specific performance or for damages, regardless of the doctrine of spousal immunity, and the defaulting party shall pay the other party's costs, expenses and attorneys' fees. This paragraph shall not require a party to execute a promissory note or other evidence of debt for the other party; but if a party executes a promissory note or other evidence of debt for the other party, that other party shall indemnify the party executing the note or other evidence of debt from any claims or demands arising from the execution of the instrument. Execution of an instrument shall not give the executing party any right or interest in the property of the party requesting execution.

17. PROPERTY DIVISION UPON DIVORCE, DISSOLUTION OF MARRIAGE, OR SEPARATION.

In the event of divorce, dissolution of marriage, or separation proceedings being filed and pursued by either party, the parties agree that the terms and provisions of this agreement shall govern all of their rights as to property; alimony including permanent periodic, rehabilitative, and lump sum; property settlement; rights of community property; and equitable distribution against the other. Each party releases and waives any claims for special equity in the other party's separate property or in jointly owned property. If either party files for alimony, or spousal support unconnected with divorce, dissolution of marriage, separation, or separate maintenance, the parties agree that the party filing said proceedings shall ask the court to follow the provisions and terms of this premarital agreement.

18. ALIMONY.

In the event divorce, dissolution of marriage, separation, or similar proceedings are filed by either party in any state or country, the parties agree that neither party will request or receive alimony or support, whether temporary, rehabilitative, permanent, or lump sum. In consideration for not requesting alimony, the ☒ Husband ❑ Wife shall pay to the other party a sum equal to $ _5,000_

for each full year of marriage up to the date a divorce, dissolution of marriage, separation, or similar action is filed. Said sum shall be paid regardless of which party files, and shall terminate on either the death or remarriage of the payee, or on the death of the payor, whichever occurs first.

GW	*MDC*

19. **CHILD SUPPORT.**

In the event of divorce, dissolution of marriage, or separation, and there are any minor children of the parties, the parties agree that each shall contribute to the support of any such children in the following proportions:

_____75_____% from the Husband.

_____25_____% from the Wife.

Such support shall continue until: Age 18, or graduation from high school, whichever occurs last, provided any such child is enrolled as a full time student and is making a good faith effort to graduate. The amount of support shall be determined by agreement of the parties. If the parties cannot agree, the amount of support shall be determined by the court. Both parties acknowledge that they are aware that the court has the ultimate authority to determine child support, taking into consideration the needs of the children and any other factors required by law to be considered.

20. **DISPOSITION UPON DEATH.**

Subject to the conditions set forth in this paragraph, the ❑ Husband ☒ Wife shall receive from the other party after his/her death, the sum of $_35,000_____, free of any and all inheritance and estate taxes, in place of, and in full and final settlement and satisfaction of, any and all rights and claims which he/she might otherwise have in the other party's estate and property under any law now or hereafter in force in this or any other jurisdiction, whether as a right of election to take against the other party's will, as an intestate share of the estate, or otherwise. The ❑ Husband ☒ Wife shall only be entitled to receive said amount if all of the following conditions are met: (1) the parties were married at the time of death, (2) he/she survives the decedent, (3) the parties were not separated at the time of death, and (4) no divorce, dissolution of marriage, or separation proceedings were in progress at the time of death. If any of the above conditions are not met, then he/she shall not be entitled to any sums from the other party's estate. Neither party intends by this agreement to release, waive, or relinquish any devise or bequest left to either by specific provision in the will or codicil of the other, any property voluntarily transferred by the other, any joint tenancy created by the other, or any right to serve as executor or personal representative of the other's estate if specifically nominated in the other's will or codicil.

_GW_		_MDC_

21. **LIFE INSURANCE.**

The parties shall maintain the following life insurance policies payable to the other party on death in the face amounts of at least:

Life insurance on the life of the Husband payable to the Wife or a person she designates of at least $__100,000__.

Life insurance on the life of the Wife payable to the Husband or a person he designates of at least $__25,000__.

22. **DEBTS.**

Neither party shall assume or become responsible for the payment of any pre-existing debts or obligations of the other party because of the marriage. Neither party shall do anything that would cause the debt or obligation of one of them to become a claim, demand, lien, or encumbrance on the other's property without the other party's written consent. If a debt or obligation of one party is asserted as a claim or demand against the other's separate property without such written consent, the party who is responsible for the debt or obligation shall indemnify the other from the claim or demand, including the payment of the other party's costs, expenses, and attorneys' fees.

23. **HOMESTEAD.**

Each party releases any claim, demand, right, or interest that the party may acquire because of the marriage in any real property of the other because of the homestead property provisions of the laws of any state concerning the descent of the property as homestead.

24. **COMMINGLING OF INCOME AND ASSETS.**

The parties recognize that it is possible for their income or assets to become, or appear to become, commingled. It is the parties' intention that any commingling of income or assets shall not be interpreted to imply any abandonment of the terms and provisions of this agreement, that the provisions contained herein regarding the parties' interests in jointly held property be applied, and that in other instances each party's interest be determined by each party's proportionate contribution toward the total funds or value of assets in question.

| GW | MDC |

25. TAX RETURNS / GIFTS / LEGAL PROCEEDINGS.

The fact that the parties may file joint local, state, or federal income tax returns, or any other joint tax papers or documents, or make gifts of property or cash to each other, or not account to each other with regard to the expenditure of income, shall not be interpreted to imply any abandonment of the terms and provisions of this agreement. The filing of a divorce, dissolution of marriage, separation, or other legal action or proceeding shall not be deemed as any abandonment of the terms and provisions of this agreement.

26. FREE AND VOLUNTARY ACT.

The parties acknowledge that executing this agreement is a free and voluntary act, and has not been entered into for any reason other that the desire for the furtherance of their relationship in marriage. Each party acknowledges that he or she has had adequate time to fully consider the consequences of signing this agreement, and has not been pressured, threatened, coerced, or unduly influenced to sign this agreement.

27. GOVERNING LAW.

This agreement shall be governed by the laws of __Virginia__ .

28. SEVERABILITY.

If any part of this agreement is adjudged invalid, illegal, or unenforceable, the remaining parts shall not be affected.

29. FURTHER ASSURANCE.

Each party shall execute any instruments or documents at any time requested by the other party that are necessary or proper to effectuate this agreement.

30. BINDING AGREEMENT / NO OTHER BENEFICIARY.

This agreement shall be binding upon the parties, and upon their heirs, executors, personal representatives, administrators, and assigns. No person shall have a right or cause of action arising or resulting from this agreement except those who are parties to it and their successors in interest.

31. RELEASE.

Except as otherwise provided in this agreement, each party releases all claims or demands to the property or estate of the other, however and whenever acquired, including acquisitions in the future.

GW   MDC

32. **ENTIRE AGREEMENT.**

This instrument, including any attached exhibits, constitutes the entire agreement of the parties. No representations or promises have been made except those that are set out in this agreement. This agreement may not be modified or terminated except in writing signed by the parties.

33. **PARAGRAPH HEADINGS.**

The headings of the paragraphs contained in this agreement are for convenience only, and are not to be considered a part of this agreement or used in determining its content or context.

34. **ATTORNEYS' FEES IN ENFORCEMENT.**

A party who fails to comply with any provision or obligation contained in this agreement shall pay the other party's attorneys' fees, costs, and other expenses reasonably incurred in enforcing this agreement and resulting from the noncompliance.

35. **SIGNATURES AND INITIALS OF PARTIES / UNMARKED BOXES.**

The signatures of the parties on this document, and their initials on each page, indicate that each party has read, and agrees with, this entire Premarital Agreement, including any and all exhibits attached hereto. Any provision containing a box, ❑ , which does not contain an "X" does not apply and is not a part of the agreement of the parties.

36. ❑ **OTHER PROVISIONS.** Additional provisions are contained in the Addendum to Premarital Agreement attached hereto and made a part hereof.

George Washington
Husband

Martha Dandridge Curtis
Wife

Executed in the presence of:

Alexander Hamilton
Name:___Alexander Hamilton___
Address:___286 Duelist Avenue___
___Washington, DC 20064___

Dolley Madison
Name:___Dolley Madison___
Address:___1642 Cupcake Lane___
___Fairfax, VA 20599___

{Notary provision omitted to save space}

LISTING ASSETS AND DEBTS

You and your partner will be required to list assets and debts on your FINANCIAL STATEMENT (Forms 3 and 4), and in each party's SCHEDULE OF SEPARATE PROPERTY (Forms 5 and 6) and SCHEDULE OF JOINT PROPERTY (Form 7). It is important to list everything, and to list it accurately and precisely. The following information is provided to help you determine what and how to list things.

CASH AND BANK ACCOUNTS
For the FINANCIAL STATEMENT, it is sufficient to just give the total from all accounts. However, for the schedules of property, list each account separately, giving the name of the bank, credit union, etc., and the account number. This includes savings and checking accounts, and certificates of deposit (CDs).

STOCKS, BONDS, NOTES, ANNUITIES, PENSIONS, AND OTHER INVESTMENTS
All stocks, bonds, or other "paper investments" should be listed. Write down the number of shares, the certificate numbers (if any), and the name of the company or other organization that issued them. Also copy any notation such as "common" or "preferred" stock or shares. This information can be obtained from the certificate itself, or from a statement from your stock broker, financial planner, issuing company or organization, etc. Such a statement should also give you a current value for your FINANCIAL STATEMENT. If you do not have an exact value as of the date you sign your FINANCIAL STATEMENT, note that it is an "approximate value," "estimated value," or "value as of _____ " (fill in the most recent date you were able to determine a value). Also list retirement or pension plans (see page 31 on pension plans).

REAL ESTATE
List each piece of property separately. The description might include a legal description (these can be quite long, and are not necessary if there is another way to clearly and unmistakably identify the property), street address for the property, a subdivision name and lot number, or anything which lets you know what piece of property you are referring to. In assigning a value to the property, consider the market value, which is how much you could probably sell the property for. This might be what

similar properties in the area have sold for recently. You might also consider how much you paid for the property, or how much the property is insured for. ***Do not*** use the tax assessment value, as this is usually considerably lower than the market value. Make a note on your FINANCIAL STATEMENT to indicate how the value was determined, such as "purchase price on _____" (fill in the date of purchase), "estimated value based on recent sales of similar property," "appraised value as of _____" (fill in the date of the appraisal), etc.

AUTOMOBILES, BOATS, AND OTHER VEHICLES

This category includes cars, trucks, motor homes, recreational vehicles (RVs), motorcycles, boats, trailers, airplanes, and any other means of transportation for which the State requires a title and registration. You should include the make, model, year and serial number. Regarding a value, you can go the the public library and ask to look at the *blue book* for cars, trucks or whatever it is you're looking for. A blue book (which may actually be any color) gives the average values for used vehicles. Your librarian can help you find what you need. Another source is to look in the classified advertising section of a newspaper to see what similar vehicles are selling for. You might also try calling a dealer to see if he can give you a rough idea of the value. Be sure you consider the condition of the vehicle.

OTHER PERSONAL PROPERTY

This general category is further broken down on the FINANCIAL STATEMENT. For each type of property listed on the form, type in an estimate of the value. Some of the items which fit in this category are discussed in more detail below.

Appliances, electronic equipment, yard machines, etc. These are such things as televisions, VCRs, refrigerators, lawn mowers and power tools. Include the make, model, serial number, size, or whatever identifying information is available. You will probably only be able to estimate the value.

Furniture. This will be included in the "Contents of home" line of the FINANCIAL STATEMENT. On the schedules of property, list furniture as specifically as possible. You should include the type of piece (such as sofa, coffee table, etc.), the color, and if you know it, the manufacturer, line name or the style. Furniture usually won't have a serial number, although if you find one be sure to write it on the list. Once again, estimate the value.

Jewelry and collections. You don't need to list individual items of inexpensive, or costume jewelry. However, if you own an expensive piece you should list it separately, along with an appraised, insured, or estimated value. Be sure to include silverware, furs, original art, gold, coin collections, etc. Again, be as detailed and specific as possible.

Recreation/sports equipment. Examples are golf clubs, guns, skis, cameras, pool tables, camping or fishing equipment. Just give a total on the FINANCIAL STATEMENT. On the schedules of property, be as specific as possible, and give an appraised, insured, or estimated value.

Trade tools/equipment. If you have tools, equipment, or other things which you use in your business or job, give a total estimated value on your FINANCIAL STATEMENT. On the schedules of property, describe these items as specifically as possible.

Life insurance. Fill in the total on the FINANCIAL STATEMENT. On the schedules of property, type in the name of the company issuing the policy, the policy number, the face amount and cash surrender value (if any), and any other information which may specifically identify the policy.

BUSINESS OWNERSHIPS AND INTERESTS
If you own a business, or any interest in a business, list the name of the company or business, describe your interest in the business (such as "sole owner," "50% active partner," "5% silent partner," "10% shareholder," etc.). Estimate the value as best as you can for your FINANCIAL STATEMENT.

OTHER ASSETS
The category for "Other Assets" is simply a general reference to anything of value that doesn't fit in one of the above categories, or that is of such a value that you feel it should be listed separately. Examples

might be a pet, portable spa, above-ground swimming pool, farm animals or machinery, etc.

FINANCIAL STATEMENT (FORMS 3 AND 4)

You and your spouse each need to complete a FINANCIAL STATEMENT. These forms must be completed accurately, and must list all of your income, assets and debts. If there is ever a challenge to the premarital agreement, your FINANCIAL STATEMENT will be your evidence that you fully disclosed your financial situation to your spouse.

The FINANCIAL STATEMENT in appendix D is designed for information on a monthly basis. If you are paid weekly, or every two weeks, you will need to convert your income to a monthly figure. To convert weekly amounts to monthly amounts, just take the weekly figure and multiply it by 4.3. (There are roughly 4.3 weeks to a month.) To convert from every two weeks, divide by 2 and then multiply by 4.3.

Most of the blanks in the FINANCIAL STATEMENT clearly indicate what information is to be filled in there; however, the following may answer some questions:

1. Type your name (or your spouse's name) in the blank in the first paragraph

2. Complete the information called for in ITEM 1 for your occupation, employer's name and address, social security number, pay period, and rate of pay. "PAY PERIOD" refers to how often you receive your paycheck, such as "weekly," "every two weeks," "twice a month," etc. "RATE OF PAY" refers to your hourly rate, or weekly, monthly, or yearly salary, whichever applies to your situation.

3. "AVERAGE GROSS MONTHLY INCOME" refers to your total income before any deductions for taxes or other items. The other items listed on the form are some of the more

common types of income other than wages or salary. Add these items (if any) to your "AVERAGE GROSS MONTHLY INCOME" and type in the total on the line for "TOTAL MONTHLY GROSS INCOME."

4. "DEDUCTIONS," refers to deductions from gross income. The items listed on the form are some of the more common deductions.

5. "TOTAL NET INCOME." To get this figure, subtract the "TOTAL DEDUCTIONS" from the "TOTAL GROSS MONTHLY INCOME."

6. "ITEM 3" on "ASSETS," is where you list everything you own. Refer to the previous section of this chapter for more information on how to list assets.

7. "ITEM 4" on "DEBTS," is where you list everything you owe. Refer to the previous section of this chapter for more information on how to list debts. In the column marked "Creditor," type in the name of the company or person you owe the debt to. This will include such creditors as Visa, Mastercard, Sears, and other credit cards with an outstanding balance, as well as mortgages, car and boat loans, student loans, etc. In the column marked "Security," type in what property secures the debt. Be as specific as possible, such as giving the VIN number of a car. Some of your debts may not be secured, such as most credit cards. In these cases, simply type in the word "Unsecured." In the column marked "Balance," type in the total amount still owed. Finally, add the amounts in the "Balance" column, and type in the total on the last line.

8. This form should be dated and signed by you (or your spouse if it is his or her FINANCIAL STATEMENT) where indicated. Next 2 copies should be made of each FINANCIAL STATEMENT. The original will be attached to the Premarital Agreement, you should keep a copy, and your spouse should keep a copy.

9. The "ACKNOWLEDGMENT OF RECEIPT" is where each of you verify that you received a copy of the other's FINANCIAL STATEMENT. The wife will complete this section on the Husband's Financial Statement, and the husband will complete this section on the Wife's FINANCIAL STATEMENT. Type in the spouse's name in the first blank. In the second blank, write in the date the spouse received a copy. The spouse would then fill in the date after the word "DATED," and sign where indicated.

SCHEDULES OF SEPARATE PROPERTY (FORMS 5 AND 6)

The SCHEDULE OF SEPARATE PROPERTY forms will be used for you and your partner to list property which will remain separate. Form 5 is for the husband's separate property, and Form 6 is for the wife's separate property. All you need to do is describe each piece of property as precisely as possible. Refer back to the subsection of this chapter on "Separate Property" for more information about how to list items here. At the bottom of each form, fill in the date, and be sure that each of you put your initials where indicated.

SCHEDULE OF JOINT PROPERTY (FORM 7)

The SCHEDULE OF JOINT PROPERTY (Form 7) is completed the same as Forms 5 and 6, except it is for property that either you or your spouse own that you want to be considered joint property. If there is no such property, simply type in the word "None." If any real estate, mobile homes, motor vehicles, or other items are to become joint property, you may also need to contact the appropriate governmental office to arrange to have the other person's name added to the title documents. Refer back to the subsections of this chapter on "Separate Property" and

"Property Acquired During Marriage" for more information about how to list items here. At the bottom of each form, fill in the date, and be sure that each of you put your initials where indicated.

EXPENSE PAYMENT SCHEDULE (FORM 8)

The EXPENSE PAYMENT SCHEDULE (Form 8) is for you and your partner to describe how you intend to pay for your living expenses. This is to be sure you are in agreement about who is to be responsible for what bills, or for what portion of each bill. This will also assist you in making out a budget, which can help to avoid financial difficulties in the future.

ADDENDUM TO PREMARITAL AGREEMENT (FORM 9)

The ADDENDUM TO PREMARITAL AGREEMENT (Form 9) is to be used to write any provisions which are not included in the main part of the agreement, or to further explain provisions of the main part of the agreement. Type in the date of your main premarital agreement in the first paragraph. Next, type in the additional provisions. At the bottom of the form, be sure that each of you put your initials where indicated.

If you are modifying or explaining a provision in the main part of your premarital agreement, refer to the paragraph number. For example: "Paragraph 17 is modified to provide that _____."

Two of the more common provisions you may want to include in your agreement, or in an addendum, relate to pension plans and businesses.

As stated earlier, one federal court has decided that only a spouse, not a fiancé, may waive pension plan rights, and only if the agreement states that all federal pension rights are being waived, and names a beneficiary. If you or your partner intend to give up pension plan rights, you may want to consult a lawyer, or use one of the following provisions:

The following provision is for both parties to waive their rights in each other's pension plan. This should be used when each party has his or her own plan.

> **WAIVER OF PENSION RIGHTS.** Each party waives any and all state and federal rights he or she may otherwise have in any pension, retirement, or profit-sharing plan of the other party. In the event of the death of either party, _____ is named as the beneficiary of the deceased Husband's plan, and _____ is named as the beneficiary of the deceased Wife's plan. Each party further agrees to execute an agreement within ____ days after the parties' marriage, whereby such rights are waived in accordance with this paragraph. Failure of one party to execute such an agreement after the parties' marriage shall entitle the other party to declare this Premarital Agreement null and void upon written notice of such declaration to the other party.

The following provision is for use where one party is giving up rights in the other's pension. In three places you will need to cross out either the word "HUSBAND" or "WIFE," whichever does not apply.

> **WAIVER OF PENSION RIGHTS.** The HUSBAND/WIFE waives any and all state and federal rights in any pension, retirement, or profit-sharing plan of the other party. In the event of the plan holder's death, _____ is named as the beneficiary of the plan. The HUSBAND/WIFE further agrees to execute an agreement within _____ days after the parties' marriage, whereby such rights are waived in accordance with this paragraph. Failure of the HUSBAND/WIFE to execute such an agreement after the parties' marriage shall entitle the other party to declare this Premarital Agreement null and void upon written notice of such declaration to the other party.

The post-marital agreement would simply use only the first sentence of the provision above. You can't force your spouse to sign a post-marital agreement, so the only protection you would have is to put some kind of penalty in the premarital agreement if he or she refuses to sign the required pension agreement. In the paragraphs above, the penalty is that you would be able to cancel the premarital agreement. However, this may actually harm you further, depending upon what is in your pre-marital agreement. An alternative would be to have your spouse give up something he or she would otherwise receive under the premarital agreement, as a penalty for refusing to sign the post-marital agreement.

Career and Business Interests

If either or both of you have a business to keep separate, you can simply list that business on the appropriate Schedule of Separate Property (Form 5 or Form 6). If one or both or you are professionals, and want to avoid the problem of having the other claim an interest in your earnings, or if you prefer to state your business interest more specifically, you may use one of the following provisions:

The following provision is for a waiver of claims on one party's business. You will need to delete the word "HUSBAND" or "WIFE," and "he" or "she," whichever does not apply.

WAIVER OF INTERESTS IN BUSINESS.

The HUSBAND/WIFE acknowledges that he/she has no interest in, and will claim no interest in, the business of the HUSBAND/WIFE known as _____, in the event of divorce, dissolution of marriage, legal separation, or death; regardless of whether there is any appreciation in said business or whether he/she provides any personal labor, services, or other contribution to said business. Nothing in this paragraph shall prevent an inter vivos or testamentary transfer of an interest in said business.

The following provision is for a waiver of an interest in one party's career. You will need to delete the word "HUSBAND" or "WIFE," and "he" or "she," whichever does not apply.

WAIVER OF INTERESTS IN BUSINESS.

The HUSBAND/WIFE acknowledges that he/she has no interest in, and will claim no interest in, the earnings and profits of the career of the HUSBAND/WIFE as _____, in the event of divorce, dissolution of marriage, or legal separation.

You may need to make variations to these provisions, or even combine them, to fit your needs. You may also wish to consult an attorney.

CHANGING OR CANCELING YOUR AGREEMENT 7

AMENDMENT TO PREMARITAL AGREEMENT (FORM 10)

A premarital agreement is not necessarily carved in stone. As long as you and your spouse agree, the agreement can be changed. As your financial situation changes, you may need to modify your agreement. You may also want to modify your agreement if you and your spouse have children together. Form 10 is to be used anytime you and your spouse want to change any of the provisions of your premarital agreement. To complete Form 10 you need to:

1. Type in the current date in the first blank of the first, unnumbered paragraph. In the second and third blanks, type in your name and your spouse's, with the husband's name first. In the third blank, type in the date of your original premarital agreement.

2. In paragraph 1, type in whatever changes you want to make.

3. Below paragraph 3, both parties need to sign (before the witnesses and notary) where indicated. Type in the name and address of the two witnesses. The notary will then complete the notary section at the bottom.

RELEASE OF PREMARITAL AGREEMENT (FORM 11)

If, for whatever reason, you and your spouse decide to cancel your premarital agreement, you can use Form 11. To complete Form 11 you need to:

1. Type in the current date in the first blank of the first, unnumbered paragraph. In the second and third blanks, type in your name and your spouse's, with the husband's name first.

2. In paragraph 2, type in the date of your original premarital agreement.

3. If any promises were made in connection with cancelling the agreement, type in an explanation of the promises after paragraph 3. If no promises were made, type in the word "None."

4. Below paragraph 5, both parties need to sign (before the witnesses and notary) where indicated. Type in the name and address of the two witnesses. The notary will then complete the notary section at the bottom.

APPENDIX A
GLOSSARY

This appendix contains a glossary of legal terms you may encounter in relation to premarital agreements, and the related areas of property ownership, probate, and divorce. If you encounter terms that are not included here, you can look them up in a legal dictionary. The most comprehensive and commonly found legal dictionary is *Black's Law Dictionary*, which should be available at your local public library or law library.

administrator or **administratrix.** A person appointed by the court to oversee distribution of the property of someone who died without leaving a will. Administrator applies to a male, and administratrix applies to a female.

alimony. In a divorce, a payment to be made by one spouse for the support of the other.

antenuptial agreement. Another name for a premarital agreement.

beneficiary. A person who receives property from a person who died, or who benefits from an agreement between two other persons.

codicil. A change or amendment to a will.

community property. Property owned by a husband and wife together in any of the following nine states: Arizona, California, Idaho, Louisiana, Nevada, New Mexico, Texas, Washington, and Wisconsin.

decedent. In probate law, the person who has died.

devise. Real property left to someone in a will.

devisee. A person who is left real property in another person's will.

elective share. The minimal portion of property which a surviving spouse is entitled to receive when the decedent leaves a will. The surviving spouse must choose, or *elect* to take what he or she was left in the will, or to take the elective share. This generally comes into play when the decedent has left little in the will to the surviving spouse, so that he or she would receive more by taking the elective share.

equitable distribution. A legal term for how property is divided in a divorce in most states. Equitable distribution is *not* used in those states with *community property* laws.

executor or **executrix.** A person appointed by the court, or by a will, to oversee distribution of the property of someone who died with a will. Executor applies to a male, and executrix applies to a female.

heir. A person who would receive property owned by a person who died without a will.

homestead. Real property where an individual or married couple had their primary residence. This is used in some states which give special rights and protection to such property against the claims of creditors or for property tax purposes. In probate law, many states allow the surviving spouse certain rights in homestead property which cannot be given away to others by a will.

intestate and **intestate share.** Someone who dies *intestate* dies without leaving a will. The *intestate share* is the portion of property a family member receives when a person dies without leaving a will. As used in appendix C of this book, the intestate share refers to the share the surviving spouse would receive if there is no will.

joint property. Property owned by a husband and wife together.

joint tenancy. A type of property ownership by two or more persons. If one owner dies, his interest in the property goes to the surviving owner or owners. Some states may require the ownership document to include the phrase "as joint tenants with rights of survivorship."

legacy. Personal property left to someone in a will.

legatee. A person who is left personal property in another person's will.

marital property. Property considered by some state laws as owned by husband and wife together.

nonmarital property. Property owned by one spouse individually, and free form claims of the other spouse.

personal property. Property that is not *real property*.

personal representative. A person appointed by the court, or will, to oversee distribution of the property of someone who died. This is a more modern trend and generally replaces the terms *administrator, administratrix, executor,* and *executrix.*

prenuptial agreement. Another name for a premarital agreement.

real property. Land and things permanently attached to the land, such as a house.

separate maintenance. Another name for alimony, used in some states.

separate property. Another name for *sole property* or *nonmarital property*, used in some states.

sole property. Another name for *separate property* or *nonmarital property*, used in some states.

spousal support. Another name for alimony, used in some states.

taking against the will. When a surviving spouse chooses to take the *elective share* of the estate, instead of taking what was left to him or her in the will.

tenancy by the entirety or **tenancy by the entireties.** A type of property ownership by a married couple. This is generally the same as joint tenancy, except that it is between spouses.

tenancy in common. A type of property ownership by two or more persons. If one owner dies, his or her interest in the property goes to his heirs or devisees; not to the other owners.

APPENDIX B
STATE LAWS

This appendix contains information about the laws of each state which have some impact on premarital agreements. The fifty states and the District of Columbia are listed in alphabetical order. Under each state's listing you will find the following headings:

THE LAW

This tells about how your state's law books are organized, and where to find the basic law regarding premarital agreements. The following subheadings may also be found:

In General. This section will give the title of the volume of books containing your state's law, and the title, chapter, article or section number of a sample provision. It will also show you how your state's laws are abbreviated. There may also be additional information to help you find the law for your state. For example, look at the listing in this appendix for Alabama. The laws of Alabama are found in the set of books called the Code of Alabama. For the example given, you would look for the volume of the Code of Alabama, which contains Title 43, then look for Chapter 8, then Section 43-8-72. This would be abbreviated "C.A. §43-8-72." "C.A." stands for Code of Alabama. "§43-8-72" stands for "Section 43-8-72," which is also "Title 43, Chapter 8, Section 72."

UPAA. This will tell you if your state uses the Uniform Premarital Agreement Act. If so, the reference for this law in your state will be given. The basic UPAA is reproduced in appendix C, although the section numbers will be different in each state. Also, be sure to check your state's UPAA, because some states have made small changes in the wording.

Misc. A few states have their own laws relating to premarital agreements, which are not the UPAA, nor are they in sections of the law relating to probate or divorce. If your state has such a law, it will be listed here. There is not a "Misc" subheading for most states.

Probate. This is where you will find the reference for any premarital agreement laws in your state's probate laws.

Divorce. This is where you will find the reference for any premarital agreement laws in your state's divorce laws.

PROBATE LAWS

This tells you where to find your state's probate laws, and gives you some basic information about probate laws relating to premarital agreements, and what kind of rights you may have in your spouse's property. This is to give you a rough idea of what you may be giving up by signing a premarital agreement, and where you can look to get the details of the law in your state. You will find the following subheadings:

In General. This gives a reference to where your state's probate laws can be found. If your state has adopted the Uniform Probate Code, the letters "UPC" will appear. For example, Alabama has adopted the Uniform Probate Code, and it begins in the Code of Alabama at Section 43-8-1.

Elective Share. This gives the reference to where you can find your state's law regarding a surviving spouse's elective share. It will also give basic information about what the elective share is for your state. For example, the elective share in Alabama is the lesser of ⅓ of the deceased spouse's estate, or all of the estate minus the surviving spouse's separate property. Of course, you would need to read the specific law to get all of the details, and to find out what is considered separate property, etc. The elective share statute is found in the Alabama Code at Section 43-8-70.

Intestate Share. This will tell you what portion of your spouse's estate you would receive if he or she died without leaving a will (providing there is no premarital agreement). For example, the surviving spouse's intestate share in Alabama is $1/2$ to all of the estate. This is typical of most states, with the range depending upon how many children or other heirs there are. The law relating to the intestate share is found in the Alabama Code at Section 43-8-41.

DIVORCE LAWS

This tells you where to find your state's divorce laws, and gives you some basic information about probate laws relating to premarital agreements, and what kind of rights you may have in your spouse's property in the event of divorce. This is to give you a rough idea of what you may be giving up by signing a premarital agreement, and where you can look to get the details of the law in your state. You will find the following subheadings:

Title of Divorce Action. This tells you what a divorce action is called in your particular state. It will either be "Divorce" or "Dissolution of Marriage," depending on how it is referred to in your state. You may want to use the proper term for your state in your premarital agreement, or keep the more all-inclusive language found in the forms in appendix C. For example, Alabama uses the term *divorce*, whereas Alaska uses the term *dissolution of marriage*.

Property. This gives you a summary of the law in your state regarding the factors used to divide property in a divorce case. It will also give a reference to where you can find this in your state's laws.

Alimony. This gives you a summary of the law in your state regarding the factors used in a divorce case to determine whether alimony should be awarded, and if so, how much alimony. It will also give a reference to where you can find this in your state's laws.

ALABAMA

The Law

In General: Code of Alabama, Title 43, Chapter 8 (C.A. §43-8-72) [Look for volume 22A].

UPAA: No.

Probate: C.A. §43-8-72 [look for volume 22A]. Standard UPC waiver provision. Allows spouse to waive elective share, homestead (C.A. §43-8-110), exempt property (§43-8-111), and family allowance (§43-8-112). Any other interest may also be waived, C.A. §§43-8-290 through 43-8-298.

Divorce: C.A. §30-4-9 [look for volume 17], which provides that: "The husband and wife may contract with each other, but all contracts into which they enter are subject to the rules of law as to contracts by and between persons standing in confidential relations." Case law indicates that if the agreement is not "fair, just and equitable" as to one party, that party must have "competent, independent advice." *Tibbs v. Anderson*, 580 So.2d 1337 (Ala. 1991). Marriage itself is sufficient consideration for a premarital agreement.

Probate Laws

In General: UPC: C.A. §43-8-1. [Look for volume 22A.]

Elective share: The lesser of $1/3$, or all minus the survivor's separate estate. C.A. §43-8-70.

Intestate share: $1/2$ to all. C.A. §43-8-41.

Divorce Laws

Title of Divorce Action: Divorce.

Property: Equitable distribution under case law. Fault may be considered. No statutory factors. Courts recognize separate property as property acquired (1) before marriage; or (2) by gift or inheritance (unless used for the benefit of both parties). See C.A. §30-4-1 on husband and wife property.

Alimony: Alimony may be awarded if the party seeking alimony has insufficient property or income for support. Factors: (1) value of each party's estate; and (2) financial condition of recipient spouse's family. C.A. §30-2-50. However, property acquired before marriage is not considered unless it was regularly used for the common benefit during the marriage. C.A. §30-2-51. Fault may limit or bar alimony altogether. C.A. §30-2-52. Alimony must terminate upon remarriage or cohabitation with a member of the opposite sex. C.A. §30-2-55.

ALASKA

The Law

In General: Alaska Statutes, Title 13, Section 13.12.213 (A.S. §13.12.213). [Look for volume 4.]

UPAA: No.

Probate: A.S. §13.12.213. Standard UPC waiver provision.

Divorce: None.

Probate Law

In General: UPC: A.S. §13.06.005. [Look for volume 4.]

Elective share: 1/3. A.S. §§13.12.201 to 13.12.214.

Intestate share: 1/2 to all. A.S. §§13.12.101 to 13.12.114.

Divorce Law

Title of Divorce Action: Divorce (standard procedure), or Dissolution of Marriage (simplified procedure).

Property: Equitable distribution. Fault is not a factor. All property acquired during marriage is marital property. Factors for dividing marital property: (1) length of marriage and parties' station in life during marriage; (2) age and health of parties; (3) each party's earning capacity, including educational background, training, employment skills, work experience, length of absence from job market, and child custodial responsibilities during the marriage; (4) each party's financial condition, including availability and cost of health insurance; (5) conduct of the parties, including whether there has been unreasonable depletion of marital assets; (6) desirability of the child custodian remaining in the marital home; (7) circumstances and necessities of the parties; (8) time and manner of acquisition of the assets; and (9) the income producing capacity of the property and the value of the property. A.S. §§25.24.160(a)(4) and 25.24.230.

Alimony: Called *maintenance*. Fault not considered. Factors: (1) length of marriage and parties' station in life during marriage; (2) age and health of parties; (3) each party's earning capacity, including educational background, training, employment skills, work experience, length of absence from job market, and child custodial responsibilities during the marriage; (4) each party's financial condition, including availability and cost of health insurance; (5) conduct of the parties, including whether there has been unreasonable depletion of marital assets; (6) property division; and (7) any other relevant factor. A.S. §25.24.160(a)(2).

ARIZONA

THE LAW

In General: Arizona Revised Statutes, Section 25-201 (A.R.S. §25-201).

UPAA: A.R.S. §25-201. [Look for volume 9.]

Probate: A.R.S. §14-2207. [Look for volume 6.] Standard UPC waiver provision.

Divorce: None.

PROBATE LAW

In General: UPC: A.R.S. §14-1102. [Look for volume 6.]

Elective share: ¹/₂ to all of decedent' separate and community property. A.R.S. §14-3101.

Intestate share: ¹/₂ to all. A.R.S. §14-2102.

DIVORCE LAW

Title of Divorce Action: Dissolution of Marriage.

Property: Community property. Fault not considered. Each party retains their "sole and separate property." In dividing property the court may consider "excessive or abnormal expenditures, destruction, concealment or fraudulent disposition of community, joint tenancy and other property held in common." No other statutory factors. A.R.S. §25-318.

Alimony: Called "maintenance." Alimony may be awarded if the party: (1) lacks sufficient property to provide for his or her reasonable needs; and (2) is unable to support self through employment, or is custodian of young child so is not required to seek employment, or lacks earning ability; or (3) contributed to spouse's education; or (4) is of an age which may preclude adequate employment and the marriage was of long duration. Amount and duration factors: (1) standard of living established during the marriage; (2) duration of marriage; (3) age, employment history, earning ability and physical and emotional condition of the party seeking alimony; (4) ability of the other party to meet his or her own needs while paying alimony; (5) comparative financial resources and earning abilities; (6) contribution of the party seeking alimony to the other's earning ability; (7) extent to which the party seeking alimony has reduced income or career opportunity for the other's benefit; (8) ability of both to contribute to the child's future educational costs; (9) financial resources of the party seeking alimony, and the ability to meet own needs; (10) time needed to acquire education and training to find appropriate employment; and (11) "excessive or abnormal expenditures, destruction, concealment or fraudulent disposition of community, joint tenancy and other property held in common." A.R.S. §25-319.

ARKANSAS

THE LAW

In General: Arkansas Code of 1987 Annotated, Title 9, Chapter 11, Section 9-11-401 (A.C.A. §9-11-401).

UPAA: A.C.A. §9-11-401). [Look for volume 6.]

Probate: None.

Divorce: None.

PROBATE LAW

In General: A.C.A. §28-1-101 ("Probate Code"). [Look for volume 29.]

Elective share: Same as intestate share; must have been married at least one year to claim. A.C.A. §28-39-401.

Intestate share: 1/3 to 1/2. A.C.A. §§28-11-301, 28-11-305, and 28-11-307.

DIVORCE LAW

Title of Divorce Action: Divorce.

Property: Equitable distribution. Non-marital property is property: (1) acquired prior to marriage; (2) acquired by gift or inheritance; (3) acquired in exchange for non-marital property; (4) designated non-marital by a valid agreement; (5) from an increase in value of, or income from, non-marital property; and (6) claims for workers' compensation, personal injuries, or social security that is for permanent disability or future medical expenses. Marital property is divided equally, unless judge includes his reasons for an unequal distribution considering: (1) length of marriage; (2) age, health and station in life of the parties; (3) occupation; (4) amount and sources or income; (5) vocational skills; (6) employability; (7) each party's estate, liabilities, and needs, and opportunity for further acquisition of capital assets and income; (8) each party's contribution to the acquisition, preservation or appreciation of marital property; and (9) federal income tax consequences. A.C.A. §9-12-315. Fault may also be considered. A.C.A. §9-12-301(6).

Alimony: No statutory factors, other than that it is to be awarded as "reasonable from the circumstances of the parties and the nature of the case." Fault may be considered. A.C.A. §9-12-312.

CALIFORNIA

THE LAW

In General: *West's* Annotated California Codes, Civil, Section 5300. (A.C.C.C. §5300). Ignore the "Title" numbers. California has several Annotated California Codes, so be sure you have the properly titled set.

UPAA: A.C.C., Civil §5300. [Look for volume 52.] Be sure you have the set marked "Civil" (not "Civil Procedure").

Probate: A.C.C., Probate, §140. Be sure you have the set marked "Probate."

Divorce: A.C.C., Civil §§4800 and 4800.1(b)(2).

PROBATE LAW

In General: A.C.C., Probate volumes.

Elective share: $^1/_2$. A.C.C., Probate §6560.

Intestate share: $^1/_2$ community and quasi-community property of deceased plus $^1/_3$ of all separate property. A.C.C., Probate §6401.

DIVORCE LAWS

Title of Divorce Action: Dissolution of Marriage.

Property: Community property. Contributions of one spouse to the education and training of the other, which substantially increases that person's earning capacity, may be reimbursed to the community property. A.C.C.C. §§4800 - 4813. The court may order arbitration if the parties cannot agree on property division. No statutory factors.

Alimony: Marital misconduct is not considered. Factors: The standard of living established during the marriage, considering: (1) the extent of each party's earning capacity to maintain the standard of living, considering marketable skills, the job market, the time and expense required for the party requesting alimony to acquire education and training, the need for retraining to acquire other more marketable skills, and the extent earning capacity was impaired by periods of unemployment during the marriage due to domestic responsibilities; (2) the extent the party seeking alimony contributed to the education, training and employment of the other; (3) the spouse's ability to pay; (4) the needs of each party, based on the standard of living; (5) the assets and debts of each party; (6) the duration of the marriage; (7) the ability of the custodial parent to earn without interfering with the best interest of the children; (8) the age and health of the parties; (9) the tax consequences; and (10) any other relevant factor. A.C.C.C. §4801.

COLORADO

THE LAW

In General: *West's* Colorado Revised Statutes Annotated, Title 14, Article 2, Section 14-2-301 (C.R.S.A. §14-2-301).

UPAA: C.R.S.A. §14-2-301. "Colorado Marital Agreement Act."

Probate: C.R.S.A. §15-11-204. Standard UPC waiver provision.

Divorce: None.

PROBATE LAWS

In General: UPC: C.R.S.A. §15-10-101 ("Colorado Probate Code").

Elective share: 5% to 50%, based on length of marriage. C.R.S.A. §15-11-201.

Intestate share: $^1/_2$ to all. C.R.S.A. §15-11-102.

DIVORCE LAWS

Title of Divorce Action: Dissolution of Marriage.

Property: Equitable distribution. Fault is not considered. Separate property includes property: (1) acquired before marriage; (2) acquired by gift or inheritance; (3) acquired in exchange for non-marital property; (4) acquired after a legal separation decree; or (5) designated separate by an written agreement of the parties. Factors in dividing marital property: (1) each party's contribution to acquisition of marital property; (2) value of separate property; (3) economic circumstances of the parties, including whether custodial party should remain in marital home; and (4) any increase or decrease in value of separate property during the marriage, and any depletion of separate property for marital purposes. C.R.S.A. §14-10-113.

Alimony: Called *maintenance*. Fault is not considered. A party may be awarded alimony if he or she: (1) lacks sufficient property to meet own needs; and (2) is unable to support self by employment, or has child custody responsibilities such that employment outside the home is inappropriate. Factors in determining amount and duration of alimony: (1) financial resources and ability of spouse seeking alimony to meet his or her own needs; (2) time needed to obtain education or training to find appropriate employment, and future earning capacity; (3) standard of living established during the marriage; (4) duration of the marriage; (5) age, physical and emotional condition of the party seeking alimony; and (6) ability of other party to meet own needs while paying alimony. C.R.S.A. §14-10-114.

CONNECTICUT

The Law

In General: Connecticut General Statutes Annotated, Title 45a, Section 45a-436(f) [C.G.S.A. §46-436(f)]. Ignore "Chapter" numbers.

UPAA: No.

Probate: C.G.S.A. §46-436(f). This law states: "The provisions of this section with regard to the statutory share of the surviving spouse in the property of the deceased spouse shall not apply to any case in which, by written contract made before or after marriage, either party has received from the other what was intended as a provision in lieu of the statutory share."

Divorce: None.

Probate Laws

In General: C.G.S.A. §45a-250.

Elective Share : Life estate in $1/3$ of the property. C.G.S.A. §45a-436.

Intestate Share: $1/2$ to all. C.G.S.A. §45a-437.

Divorce Laws

Title of Divorce Action: Dissolution of Marriage.

Property: Equitable distribution. Factors: (1) length of the marriage; (2) causes of the divorce; (3) age and health of the parties, occupation, vocational skills, and employability of the parties, amount and sources of each party's income, each spouse's needs, estate, liabilities, and prospects for further acquisition of assets and income; (4) contribution of each spouse to the acquisition, preservation or appreciation of assets. C.G.S.A. §46b-81.

Alimony: Factors: (1) length of marriage; (2) cause of divorce; (3) age, health, station, occupation, amount and sources of income, vocational skills, employability, estate, and needs of each party; and (4) property division; and (5) desirability of child custodian remaining in marital home. C.G.S.A. §46b-82.

DELAWARE

The Law

In General: Delaware Code Annotated, Title 12, Section 905 (D.C.A. 12 §905).

UPAA: No.

Probate: D.C.A. 12 §905. [Look for volume 7.] Standard UPC-type waiver provision.

Divorce: D.C.A. 13 §301. [Look for volume 8.] Requires two witnesses, and agreement must be signed at least 10 days before the marriage. If the signatures are notarized, the agreement may be recorded.

Probate Laws

In General: D.C.A. 12 §101. [Look for volume 7.]

Elective share: $^{1}/_{3}$. D.C.A. 12 §§901 to 908.

Intestate share: $^{1}/_{2}$ personal property and life estate in real property, to all. D.C.A. 12 §502.

Divorce Laws

Title of Divorce Action: Divorce.

Property: Equitable distribution. Nonmarital property includes property: (1) acquired before marriage; (2) acquired after marriage if acquired by inheritance, or in exchange for other nonmarital property; and (3) by written agreement. Fault not considered. Factors: (1) length of the marriage; (2) any prior marriages; (3) each party's age, health, station, amount and sources of income, vocational skills, employability, estate, liabilities and needs; and (4) whether property award is in lieu of, or in addition to, alimony; (5) each party's opportunity for future acquisition of assets and income; (6) contribution or dissipation of assets, including as homemaker or husband; (7) value of separate property; (8) economic circumstances of each party, including whether the custodial parent should remain in the marital home; (9) whether property was acquired as a gift; (10) each party's debts; and (11) tax consequences. D.C.A. 13 §1513.

Alimony: Marriage for less than 20 years: alimony limited to a time period of 50% of the length of marriage. Marriage of 20 years or more: no limit. Fault is not a factor. Spouse seeking alimony must be (1) dependent upon spouse; (2) lack sufficient property for his or her needs; and (3) unable to support self through employment, or is not required to seek employment because he or she has child custody which makes employment inappropriate. The amount is determined by the following factors: (1) financial resources and ability to meet needs of the party seeking alimony; (2) time and expense required to acquire education and training for employment; (3) standard of living established during the marriage; (4) duration of the marriage; (5) age, physical and emotional condition of each party; (6) contribution of the party seeking alimony to the other's career; (7) ability of the other party to pay and meet his or her own needs; (8) tax consequences; (9) whether either party has foregone or postponed education and career opportunities during the marriage; and (10) any other relevant factor. D.C.A. 13 §1512.

DISTRICT OF COLUMBIA

THE LAW

In General: District of Columbia Code, Title 19, Section 113(f) [D.C.C. §19-113(f)].

UPAA: No.

Probate: D.C.C. §19-113(f). [Look for volume 5.] This law states: "A valid antenuptial or post-nuptial agreement entered into by the spouses determines the rights of the surviving spouse in the real and personal estate of the deceased spouse and the administration thereof, but a spouse may accept the benefits of a devise or bequest made to him by the deceased spouse."

Divorce: D.C.C. §16-910. [Look for volume 5.] This law provides for how property is to be divided "…in the absence of a valid ante-nuptial agreement…"

PROBATE LAWS

In General: D.C.C. §18-101. [Look for volume 5.]

Elective Share: Basically $\frac{1}{2}$, although the statute is more complex. D.C.C. §19-113(e).

Intestate Share: $\frac{1}{2}$ to all. D.C.C. §§19-302 and 19-305.

DIVORCE LAWS

Title of Divorce Action: Divorce.

Property: Equitable distribution. Fault is not a factor. "Sole property" is property (1) acquired before marriage; (2) acquired by gift or inheritance; (3) acquired in exchange for such property; and (4) increased value of sole property. Marital property divided according to following factors: (1) duration of the marriage; (2) any prior marriages; (3) each party's age, health, occupation, amount and sources of income, vocational skills, and employability; (4) each party's assets, debts and needs; (5) child custody provisions; (6) whether property division is in lieu of or in addition to alimony; (7) each party's opportunity for future acquisition of assets and income; (8) each party's contribution to the acquisition, preservation, appreciation, dissipation, or depreciation of marital assets; (9) each party's contribution as a homemaker or to the family unit; and (10) any other relevant factor. D.C.C. §16-910.

Alimony: Fault may be considered. Statute merely states that alimony may be awarded "if it seems just and proper." D.C.C. §§16-912 and 16-913. No other statutory factors or guidelines.

FLORIDA

THE LAW

In General: Florida Statutes, Chapter 732, Section 732.702 (F.S. §732.702).

UPAA: No.

Probate: F.S. §732.702. Similar to standard UPC-type waiver provision.

Divorce: None.

PROBATE LAWS

In General: F.S. §§731.005 to 735.302.

Elective Share: 30%, but statute is somewhat more complex. F.S. §732.207.

Intestate Share: ¹/₂ to all. F.S. §732.102.

DIVORCE LAWS

Title of Divorce Action: Dissolution of Marriage.

Property: Equitable distribution. Fault is not considered. A "special equity" claim for nonmarital property must be included in the petition. Nonmarital property is property: (1) acquired before marriage; (2) acquired by gift or inheritance; (3) designated nonmarital in an agreement between the parties; (4) acquired in exchange for property in (1), (2), or (3) above; and (5) income from nonmarital property, unless the parties treated or used it as marital income. F.S. §61.075(5). Marital property includes all retirement, profit-sharing, and deferred compensation plans. F.S.§61.076. Marital property divided considering: (1) each party's contribution to the marriage; (2) each party's economic circumstances; (3) duration of the marriage; (4) either party's interruption of personal career or educational opportunities; (5) either party's contribution to the personal career or educational opportunities of the other; (6) desirability of retaining any asset intact and free of any claim of or interference from the other; (7) each party's contribution to the acquisition, enhancement, and production on income or the improvement of both marital and nonmarital property; (8) desirability for the custodial parent to remain in the marital home; and (9) any other relevant factor. F.S. §61.075.

Alimony: Factors: (1) adultery; (2) standard of living established during marriage; (3) duration of marriage; (4) each party's age, physical and emotional condition; (5) each party's financial resources, and the marital and nonmarital property distribution; (6) time needed to acquire sufficient education and training to find appropriate employment; (7) each party's contribution to the marriage; (8) all sources of income available; and (9) any other relevant factor. F.S. §61.08.

GEORGIA

The Law

In General: Official Code of Georgia Annotated, Title 19, Chapter 3, Section 19-13-62. (C.G.A. §19-33-62). This is not the "Georgia Code," which is a separate, outdated set of books with a completely different numbering system. If all you can find is the Georgia Code, look for a cross-reference table to the Official Code of Georgia.

UPAA: No.

Probate: Spouse may renounce rights, C.G.A. §53-2-115. These include those rights under C.G.A. §§53-2-10 (limit on gifts to charity), 53-5-1 (elective share of 1 year's support), and 53-4-2 (share of intestate estate).

Divorce: C.G.A. §§19-33-62 to 19-13-68. [Look for volume 16.] Requires two witnesses. C.G.A. §19-3-63.

Probate Laws

In General: C.G.A. §53-1-1. [Look for volume 40.]

Elective Share: One year's support. C.G.A. §53-5-1.

Intestate Share: ¹/₄ to all. C.G.A. §53-4-2.

Divorce Laws

Title of Divorce Action: Divorce.

Property: Equitable distribution. No factors in statute.

Alimony: To qualify for alimony, proof of the cause of the divorce must be presented. Desertion or adultery is a bar to alimony. See C.G.A. §19-6-1. The amount is based upon the need of the party seeking alimony and the other party's ability to pay, considering: (1) standard of living established during the marriage; (2) duration of the marriage; (3) age, physical and emotional condition of the parties; (4) financial resources of each party; (5) time needed to acquire education and training to obtain employment; (6) contribution of each party to the marriage; (7) condition of the parties, including the separate estate, earning capacity and fixed liabilities; and (8) any other relevant factor. C.G.A. §19-6-5.

HAWAII

THE LAW

In General: Hawaii Revised Statutes, Title 572D, Section 572D-1 (H.R.S. §572D-1). [Look for volume 12A.] Ignore "Title" numbers.

UPAA: H.R.S. §572D-1.

Probate: H.R.S. §560:2-204. Standard UPC waiver provision.

Divorce: None.

PROBATE LAWS

In General: UPC: H.R.S. §560:1-101. [Look for volume 12A.]

Elective Share: ⅓. H.R.S. §560:2-201.

Intestate Share: ½ to all. H.R.S. §560:2-102.

DIVORCE LAWS

Title of Divorce Action: Divorce.

Property: Equitable distribution. Factors: (1) respective merits of the parties; (2) relative abilities of the parties; (3) condition each party will be in after divorce; (4) burdens imposed on either spouse for the benefit of the children; and (5) any other relevant circumstances. H.R.S. §580-47.

Alimony: Called *spousal support and maintenance*. Marital misconduct is not considered. Factors: (1) each party's financial resources; (2) ability of party seeking alimony to meet own needs; (3) duration of marriage; (4) standard of living established during marriage; (5) ages of parties; (6) each party's physical and emotional condition; (7) each party's usual occupation during the marriage; (8) vocational skills and employability of party seeking alimony; (9) needs of the parties; (10) either party's child custodial and support responsibilities; (11) ability of party to pay alimony and meet own needs; (12) condition each party will be in after divorce; (13) probable duration of the need for alimony; and (14) any other relevant factor. H.R.S. §580-47.

IDAHO

The Law

In General: Idaho Code, Title 15, Section 15-2-208 (I.C. §15-2-208). [Look for volume 3.]

UPAA: No.

Probate: I.C. §15-2-208). [Look for volume 3.] Standard UPC waiver provision.

Divorce: I.C. §32-916. [Look for volume 6.] This law states: "The property rights of husband and wife are governed by this chapter, unless there is a marriage settlement agreement entered into prior to or during marriage containing stipulations contrary thereto."

Probate Laws

In General: UPC: I.C. §15-1-101. [Look for volume 3.]

Elective Share: ¹/₂. I.C. §15-2-203.

Intestate Share: ¹/₂ community property of deceased plus 1/2 to all of separate property. I.C. §15-2-102.

Divorce Laws

Title of Divorce Action: Divorce.

Property: Community property. Separate property is property acquired: (1) before marriage; (2) by gift or inheritance; and (3) as proceeds of separate property and acquired with proceeds of separate property. I.C. §32-903. Marital property is to be divided equally, unless judge gives reasons based upon: (1) duration of marriage; (2) any premarital agreement; (3) each party's age, health, occupation, amount and sources of income, vocational skills, employability, and liabilities; (4) each party's needs; (5) whether property division is in lieu of or in addition to alimony; (6) each party's present and potential earning capacity; and (7) each party's retirement benefits, including social security, civil service, military and railroad pensions. I.C. §§32-712.

Alimony: Called *separate maintenance*. Either party may be awarded alimony if he or she: (1) lacks sufficient property to be self-supporting; and (2) is unable to be self-supporting through employment. Factors for determining amount and duration: (1) financial resources of the party seeking alimony, including property awarded and ability to meet own needs; (2) time needed to acquire education and training to become employed; (3) duration of marriage; (4) age, physical and emotional condition of party seeking alimony; (5) ability of party paying alimony to meet own needs while paying; (6) tax consequences; (7) fault of either party; and (8) any other relevant factor. I.C. §32-705.

ILLINOIS

THE LAW

In General: There are two sets of books containing the laws of Illinois; references are given to both. Smith-Hurd Illinois Annotated Statutes, Chapter 40, Paragraph 2601 (I.A.S. 40 ¶2601); *West's* Smith-Hurd Illinois Compiled Statutes Annotated, Chapter 750, Act 10, Article 1 (750 ILCS 10/1).

UPAA: I.A.S. 40 ¶2601; 750 ILCS 10/1. Known as the "Illinois Uniform Premarital Agreement Act."

Probate: None.

Divorce: None.

PROBATE LAWS

In General: I.A.S. 110 1/2 ¶1-1; 755 ILCS 5/1-1. Known as the "Probate Act of 1975."

Elective Share: $^1/_2$ if no children; $^1/_3$ if children. I.A.S. 110 1/2 ¶2-8; 755 ILCS 5/2-8. Also, 9 months of support; which shall be not less than $10,000 plus $5,000 for each child. I.A.S. 110 1/2 ¶15-1; 755 ILCS 5/15-1.

Intestate Share: $^1/_2$ to all. I.A.S. 110 1/2 ¶2-1; 755 ILCS 5/2-1.

DIVORCE LAWS

Title of Divorce Action: Dissolution of Marriage.

Property: Equitable distribution. Fault is not considered. Nonmarital property is property: (1) acquired before marriage; (2) acquired after marriage by gift, inheritance, in exchange for other nonmarital property, or after a legal separation; (3) designated nonmarital by written agreement of the parties; (4) designated nonmarital by a judgment from the spouse; or (5) increased value or income from property in (1) through (4). Division of marital property based on following factors: (1) contribution or dissipation of each party; (2) value of separate property; (3) duration of the marriage; (4) economic circumstances of the parties, including whether custodial parent should remain in marital home; (5) prior marriage obligations; (6) any pre-marital agreements; (7) age, health, station, occupation, income, skills, employability, estate, liabilities, and needs of each party; (8) child custody provisions; (9) whether property is in lieu of, or in addition to, alimony; (10) each party's opportunity for future acquisition of assets and income; and (11) tax consequences. I.S.A. 40 ¶503; 750 ILCS 5/503.

Alimony: Fault is not considered. To qualify for alimony the person seeking it must (1) lack property to provide for his or her self; (2) be unable to be self-supporting through employment, or not required to work due to child care responsibilities; and (3) be otherwise without sufficient income. If qualified, the following factors determine the amount and duration: (1) each party's financial resources; (2) time required to acquire education and training to become employable; (3) standard of living established during the marriage; (4) duration of the marriage; (5) age, physical and emotional condition of each party; (6) the payor's ability to pay and meet his or her own expenses; and (7) tax consequences of the property division. I.S.A. 40 ¶504; 750 ILCS 5/504.

INDIANA

THE LAW

In General: *West's* Annotated Indiana Code, Title 29, Article 1, Chapter 2, Section 13 (A.I.C. §29-1-2-13).

UPAA: No.

Probate: A.I.C. §29-1-2-13. Similar to standard UPC-type waiver provision. A.I.C. §§29-1-2-13 and 29-1-3-6.

Divorce: A.I.C. §31-1-11.5-10. Specifically authorizes and encourages agreements as to alimony, property, and custody and support of children.

PROBATE LAWS

In General: A.I.C. §29-1-1-1. Known as the "Probate Code," which somewhat follows UPC.

Elective Share: $^1/_3$ to $^3/_4$. See A.I.C. §29-1-3-1 for details.

Intestate Share: Life estate in real property and $^1/_3$ personal property, to all. A.I.C. §29-1-2-1.

DIVORCE LAWS

Title of Divorce Action: Dissolution of Marriage.

Property: Equitable distribution. Fault is not a factor. Property acquired before marriage is a part of the marital estate, although time of acquisition is a factor to be considered in dividing the property. Equal division is presumed. actors considered in unequal distribution claim are: (1) contribution of each party to acquisition; (2) extent of property acquired prior to marriage, or by gift or inheritance; (3) economic circumstances at the time of distribution, including whether custodial parent should remain in marital home; (4) conduct of the parties as related to disposition or dissipation of assets; (5) the earnings, or earning capacity, of each party; and (6) tax consequences. If insufficient marital property, court may award money to party for contribution to the other's education. See A.I.C. §31-1-11.5-11.

Alimony: Fault is not a factor. Alimony may be awarded for a necessary period of time if (1) the party seeking alimony is physically or mentally incapacitated; or (2) lacks financial ability and is custodian of a physically or mentally incapacitated child which requires that party to forego employment. Rehabilitative alimony for up to 3 years may be awarded after considering: (1) each party's educational level at the time of the marriage and at the time the petition was filed; (2) whether the party seeking alimony had his or her education, training or employment interrupted due to homemaking or child care responsibilities; (3) earning capacity of each party; and (4) time and expense required to acquire education and training to obtain employment. A.I.C. §31-1-11.5-11.

IOWA

THE LAW

In General: Iowa Code Annotated, Section 596.1 (I.C.A. §596.1).

UPAA: I.C.A. §596.1. [Look for volume 39, 1992 Cumulative Annual Pocket Part.]

Probate: None.

Divorce: None.

PROBATE LAWS

In General: I.C.A. §633.1. Known as the "Iowa Probate Code."

Elective Share: $^1/_3$, plus all of personal property of the decedent as head of family that is exempt from execution by creditors. I.C.A. §633.238.

Intestate Share: Greater of $^1/_2$ or $50,000, to all. I.C.A. §§633.211 and 633.212.

DIVORCE LAWS

Title of Divorce Action: Dissolution of Marriage.

Property: Equitable distribution. Fault is not considered. Separate property is property acquired: (1) by inheritance or gift; or (2) before marriage. Marital property divided considering: (1) length of marriage; (2) property brought into the marriage; (3) each party's contribution to the marriage; (4) each party's age, physical and emotional health; (5) either party's contribution to the other's education, training, and increased earning power; and (6) each party's earning capacity, including educational background, training, employment skills, work experience, length of absence from job market, child custodial responsibilities, and time and expense needed to acquire education and training to become self-supporting at the standard of living established during the marriage; (7) desirability of custodial party remaining in marital home; (8) amount and duration of alimony, and whether property division should be in lieu of or in addition to alimony; (9) each party's other economic circumstances, including pension benefits; (10) tax consequences; (11) any written agreements of the parties; and (11) any other relevant factor. I.C.A. §598.21.

Alimony: Factors: (1) length of marriage; (2) age and physical and emotional health of the parties; (3) property distribution; (4) educational level of each party at time of marriage and at time petition is filed; (5) earning capacity of party seeking alimony, including educational background, training, employment skills, work experience, length of absence from job market, child custodial responsibilities, and time and expense needed to acquire education and training to find appropriate employment; (6) the feasibility of the party seeking alimony becoming self-supporting at a standard of living reasonably comparable to that during marriage, and length of time needed to do so; (7) tax consequences; (8) any agreements between the parties; and (9) any other relevant factors. I.C.A. §§598.21.

KANSAS

THE LAW

In General: Kansas Statutes Annotated, Section 23-801 (K.S.A. §23-801). [Look for the set of books titled "Kansas Statutes Annotated, Official."] Any recent changes can be found in a soft-cover separate volume supplement. Avoid the set titled "*Vernon's* Kansas Statutes Annotated," or ask the librarian for assistance if this is all you can find. Both sets have very poor indexing systems.

UPAA: K.S.A. §23-801. [Look for volume 2A, page 566. This will be a 1988 edition, published by *Ensley*, and will say "Courts to Domestic Relations" on the cover.]

Probate: None.

Divorce: None.

PROBATE LAWS

In General: K.S.A. §59-101.

Elective Share: ¹/₂ to all, depending upon the number of children. K.S.A. §§59-504 and 59-603.

Intestate Share: ¹/₂ to all. K.S.A. §59-504.

DIVORCE LAWS

Title of Divorce Action: Divorce.

Property: Equitable distribution. All property is marital property. Factors for division: (1) age of parties; (2) duration of marriage; (3) property owned by the parties; (4) each party's present and future earning capacity; (5) time, source and manner of acquisition of the property; (6) family ties and obligations; (7) any award of alimony or lack thereof; (8) any dissipation of assets; and (9) any other relevant factor. K.S.A. §60-1610(b)(1).

Alimony: Called *maintenance*. Limited to 121 months, with one application for 121 month extension. Fault not considered. No statutory factors other than "in an amount the court finds to be fair, just and equitable under all of the circumstances." Payment must be through court clerk or court trustee. K.S.A. §60-1610(b)(2).

KENTUCKY

THE LAW

In General: Kentucky Revised Statutes, Section 371.010(5) (K.R.S. §§371.010(5).

UPAA: No.

Misc: K.R.S. §§371.010(5) and 382.080. [Look for volume 13, Part 2.] These statutes simply refer to "agreements in consideration of marriage," thereby implying that they are acceptable in Kentucky.

Probate: None.

Divorce: None.

PROBATE LAWS

In General: K.R.S. §§391.010 to 397.080. [Look for volume 14.]

Elective Share: $^1/_3$ to $^1/_2$. K.R.S. §§392.020 and 392.080.

Intestate Share: $7,500 in personal property to all. K.R.S. §§391.010 to 391.030.

DIVORCE LAWS

Title of Divorce Action: Dissolution of Marriage.

Property: Equitable distribution. Non-marital property is property acquired (1) before marriage; (2) by gift, or inheritance; (3) in exchange for such property; (4) after a legal separation; (5) property set forth as non-marital in a written agreement; and (6) the increase in value of pre-marriage property, unless the increase in value is due to the efforts of the other party. Also, if one party's retirement benefits are non-marital, so are the other's. Marital misconduct not considered. Division of marital property is determined by the following factors: (1) contribution of each party to the acquisition; (2) value of separate property; (3) duration of the marriage; and (4) economic circumstances of the parties, including whether the custodial parent should remain in the marital home. K.R.S. §403.190.

Alimony: Fault is not considered. Alimony is only permitted if the person seeking alimony (1) lacks sufficient property to provide for his or her needs; and (2) is unable to be self-supporting through employment, or is custodian of a child whose condition or circumstances make it appropriate not to seek outside employment. Once eligible, the amount is determined by considering the following factors: (1) financial resources of the person seeking alimony; (2) time needed to acquire education and training to become employable; (3) standard of living established during the marriage; (4) duration of the marriage; (5) age, physical and emotional condition of the person seeking alimony; and (6) the ability of the payor to meet his or her own needs while paying alimony. K.R.S. §403.200.

LOUISIANA

THE LAW

In General: *West's* LSA, Civil Code, Article 2328 (L.S.A., Civil Code, Art. 2328). "LSA" stands for "Louisiana Statutes Annotated." These are divided into sets of volumes titled "Revised Statutes," "Civil Code," "Civil Procedure," and "Criminal Procedure," so be sure you locate the correct set.

UPAA: No.

Probate: L.S.A., Civil Code, Art. 1734.

Divorce: None.

Misc.: L.S.A., Civil Code, Art. 2328, which provides: "A matrimonial agreement is a contract establishing a regime of separation of property or modifying or terminating the legal regime. Spouses are free to establish by matrimonial agreement a regime of separation of property or modify the legal regime as provided by law. The provisions of the legal regime that have not been excluded or modified by agreement retain their force and effect." See also LSA, Civil Code, Art. 1734 through 1742 regarding "donations by marriage contract."

PROBATE LAWS

In General: L.S.A., Civil Code, Art. 1467.

Elective Share: None (but survivor gets ½ of community property estate and all of his or her separate estate).

Intestate Share: Use of (called *usufruct*) community property, to all. L.S.A., Civil Code, Art. 888 through 894.

DIVORCE LAWS

Title of Divorce Action: Divorce.

Property: Community property. No factors in statute. Although not considered a part of the marital property, it is possible to obtain an award for financial contributions to a spouse's education and training that increased the spouse's earning power, "to the extent that the claimant did not benefit during the marriage from the increased earning power." C.C., Art. 121.

Alimony: Permanent alimony may only be awarded to a spouse without fault and without sufficient means of support. Limited to one-third of the payor's income. Amount determined by following factors: (1) each party's income, means and assets; (2) liquidity of assets; (3) financial obligations and earning capacity; (4) effect of child custody on earning capacity; (5) time needed to acquire education, training or employment; (6) health and age of the parties, and any child support obligations; and (7) any other factor the judge decides is relevant. C.C., Art. 160.

MAINE

The Law

In General: Maine Revised Statutes Annotated, Title 19, Section 141 (19 M.R.S.A. §141).

UPAA: 19 M.R.S.A. §141.

Probate: None.

Divorce: None.

Probate Laws

In General: UPC: 18A M.R.S.A. §1-101. Known as the "Probate Code." [Look for volume 10.]

Elective share: $^1/_3$ to all. 18A M.R.S.A. §§2-201 and 2-301.

Intestate Share: $^1/_2$ to all. 18A M.R.S.A. §2-102.

Divorce Laws

Title of Divorce Action: Divorce.

Property: Equitable distribution. Fault not considered. Separate property is property: (1) acquired before marriage; (2) acquired by gift or inheritance; (3) acquired in exchange for separate property; (4) acquired after a decree of legal separation; (5) designated separate by agreement of the parties; or (6) increased value of separate property. Marital property is divided considering: (1) each party's contribution to acquisition; (2) value of each party's separate property; and (3) the parties' economic circumstances at the time of division, including whether the child custodian should remain in the marital home. 19 M.R.S.A. §722-A.

Alimony: Court may award real estate to a party for life as alimony. Fault is not considered. Factors: (1) length of marriage; (2) ability of each to pay; (3) each party's age; (4) each party's employment history and employment potential; (5) each party's income; (6) each party's education and training; (7) provisions for retirement and health insurance benefits; (8) tax consequences of the property division; (9) each party's health and disabilities; (10) tax consequences of alimony; (11) either party's contribution as homemaker; (12) either party's contribution to the other's education or earning potential; (13) either party's economic misconduct resulting in the diminution of marital property or income; (14) standard of living established during marriage; and (15) any other relevant factor. 19 M.R.S.A. §721.

MARYLAND

The Law

In General: Annotated Code of Maryland, Estates and Trusts, Section 3-205 (A.C.M., Estates & Trusts, §3-205). [These volumes are arranged by subject, so be sure you have the volume marked for the subject you want, such as "Estates and Trusts," or "Family Law."]

UPAA: No.

Probate: A.C.M., Estates & Trusts, §3-205). [Be sure you have the volume marked "Estates and Trusts."] Similar to the standard UPC-type waiver provision.

Divorce: A.C.M., Family Law, §§4-204 and 8-101. [Be sure you have the volume marked "Family Law."] Section 4-204 merely states that a wife may enter into contracts with her husband. Section 8-101 states: "A husband and wife may make a valid and enforceable deed or agreement that relates to alimony, support, property rights, or personal rights."

Probate Laws

In General: A.C.M., Estates & Trusts, §1-101.

Elective Share: ¹/₃ to ¹/₂. A.C.M., Estates & Trusts, §3-203.

Intestate Share: ¹/₂ to all. A.C.M., Estates & Trusts, §3-102.

Divorce Laws

Title of Divorce Action: Divorce.

Property: Equitable distribution. Marital property does not include property (1) acquired before marriage; (2) acquired by gift or inheritance; and (3) directly traceable to property acquired before marriage, by gift, or inheritance. Marital property divided considering following factors: (1) contributions of each party to the well-being of the family; (2) value of all property interests; (3) economic circumstances of each; (4) circumstances contributing to the divorce; (5) duration of the marriage; (6) ages of the parties; (7) physical and mental condition of the parties; (8) how and when property was acquired, and the efforts of each party to acquire the property; (9) any award of alimony or use of marital home; (10) any other factor the judge considers proper. A.C.M., Family Law §§8-201, 8-203 & 8-205.

Alimony: Factors: (1) ability of the person seeking alimony to be self-supporting; (2) time needed to gain sufficient education and training; (3) standard of living established during the marriage; (4) duration of the marriage; (5) contributions of each to the well-being of the family; (6) circumstances contributing to the divorce; (7) age of the parties; (8) physical and mental condition of the parties; (9) ability of the payor to meet his or her own needs while paying alimony; (10) any agreement of the parties; (11) financial needs of the parties, including income and assets, property award, nature and amount of financial obligations, and rights to retirement benefits. Generally limited to rehabilitative period, but indefinite alimony may be awarded if (1) it is not reasonable to expect progress due to age, illness, infirmity or disability; or (2) after all progress has been made, the standard of living of the parties will be unconscionably disparate. A.C.M., Family Law §11-106.

MASSACHUSETTS

THE LAW

In General: Annotated Laws of Massachusetts, Chapter 209, Section 3 (A.L.M., C.209 §3).

UPAA: No.

Probate: None.

Divorce: None.

Misc.: A.L.M., C.209 §3, which provides: "Transfers of real and personal property between husband and wife shall be valid to the same extent as if they were sole." A.L.M., C.209 §25, which provides that a premarital agreement is void as to third parties unless it is recorded before, or within 90 days after, the marriage.

PROBATE LAWS

In General: A.L.M, Chapters 190 through 206.

Elective Share: $^1/_3$ to $25,000 plus $^1/_3$ the residue. A.L.M., C.191 §15.

Intestate Share: $^1/_2$ to all. A.L.M., C.190 §1.

Misc.: Massachusetts residents can adopt the standard will under the "Massachusetts Uniform Statutory Will Act," which gives a surviving spouse $^1/_2$ to all. A.L.M., C.191B §5.

DIVORCE LAWS

Title of Divorce Action: Divorce.

Property: Equitable distribution. Factors: (1) length of marriage; (2) conduct of parties during the marriage; (3) age, health, station, occupation, amount and sources of income, vocational skills, employability, estate, liabilities and needs of each; (4) opportunity for future acquisition of capital assets and income; (5) present and future needs of dependent children; (6) contribution of each to acquisition, preservation or appreciation of the property. A.L.M. , C. 208 §§1A & 34.

Alimony: Same factors as for property. A.L.M., C. 208 §§1A & 34.

MICHIGAN

THE LAW

In General: Michigan has two official sets of laws, each from a different publisher. One set is Michigan Statutes Annotated (abbreviated "M.S.A."), and the other is Michigan Compiled Laws Annotated (abbreviated "M.C.L.A.") Each has a completely different numbering system, although the wording of the laws will be the same. References are given to both sets as most libraries will only have one set. Ignore the volume and chapter numbers, and look for the section numbers.

UPAA: No.

Misc: Laws relating to premarital agreements are found in: Michigan Statutes Annotated, Section 26.244 (M.S.A. §26.244); and Michigan Compiled Laws Annotated, Sections 557.28 (M.C.L.A. §557.28). This section states: "A contract relating to property made between persons in contemplation of marriage shall remain in full force after marriage takes place."

Probate: M.S.A. §27.5291; M.C.L.A. §700.291. Standard UPC-type waiver provision.

Divorce: None.

PROBATE LAWS

In General: M.S.A. §27.5001; M.C.L.A. §700.1.

Elective Share: 1/2. M.S.A. §27.5282; M.C.L.A. §700.282.

Intestate Share: 1/2 to all. M.S.A. §27.5105; M.C.L.A. §700.105.

DIVORCE LAWS

Title of Divorce Action: Divorce.

Property: Equitable distribution. Vested pension benefits accumulated during the marriage are marital assets. M.S.A. §25.98; M.C.L.A. §552.18 No specific criteria are listed in the statute; only that the property will be divided as the judge "shall deem just and reasonable." M.S.A. §25.99; M.C.L.A. §§552.19.

Alimony: Alimony may be awarded if "the estate and effects awarded . . . are insufficient for the suitable support and maintenance of either party and any children of the marriage as are committed to the care and custody of either party." The amount will be determined "as the court considers just and reasonable, after considering the ability of either to pay and the character and situation of the parties, and all the other circumstances of the case." M.S.A. §25.103; M.C.L.A. §552.23.

MINNESOTA

The Law

In General: Minnesota Statutes Annotated, Section 519.11 (M.S.A. §519.11).

UPAA: No.

Misc: M.S.A. §519.11. [Look for volume 31.] Law requires full and fair disclosure of the earnings and property of each party, and that the parties have had an opportunity to consult with legal counsel of their own choice. Also requires two witnesses, and signature before a notary. Agreement must be signed prior to the day of the marriage.

Probate: M.S.A. §524.2-204. Requires that provisions of M.S.A. §519.11 be followed.

Divorce: None.

Probate Laws

In General: UPC: M.S.A. §524.1-101. [Look for volume 31A.]

Elective Share: ¹/₃. M.S.A. §524.2-201.

Intestate Share: ¹/₂ to all. M.S.A. §524.2-102.

Divorce Laws

Title of Divorce Action: Dissolution of Marriage.

Property: Equitable distribution. Fault not considered. Nonmarital property is property: (1) acquired before marriage; (2) acquired by gift or inheritance; (3) acquired in exchange for or increase in value of nonmarital property; (4) acquired after the valuation date (date of the prehearing settlement conference); or (5) designated in prenuptial agreement. M.S.A. §518.54. Factors for dividing marital property: (1) length of marriage; (2) prior marriages; (3) each party's age, health, station, occupation, amount and sources of income, vocational skills, employability, estate, liabilities, and needs; (4) each party's opportunity for future acquisition of capital assets; (5) each party's income; and (6) each party's contribution to acquisition, preservation, depreciation or appreciation of assets. There is a conclusive presumption that both parties contributed substantially to the acquisition of property and income during the time they lived together as husband and wife. M.S.A. §518.58.

Alimony: Called "maintenance." Fault not considered. Either party may be awarded if he or she: (1) lacks sufficient property to meet own needs; or (2) is unable to be self-supporting through employment, or is not required to seek employment due to responsibilities as child custodian. Amount and duration of alimony determined by: (1) financial resources of party seeking alimony; (2) time needed for education and training to find appropriate employment; (3) standard of living established during the marriage; (4) duration of the marriage, and, for a homemaker, the length of absence from employment and the extent education, skills or experience have become outmoded and earning capacity permanently diminished; (5) any loss of earnings, seniority, retirement benefits, or other employment opportunities foregone; (6) age, physical and emotional condition of the party seeking alimony; (7) ability of the other party to meet own needs while paying alimony; and (8) either party's contribution to acquisition, preservation, depreciation, or appreciation of marital property, and in furtherance of the other's employment or business. M.S.A. §518.54.

MISSISSIPPI

THE LAW

In General: Mississippi Code 1972 Annotated, Section 91-1-1 (M.C. §91-1-1). There are no laws relating to premarital agreements in Mississippi.

UPAA: No.

Probate: None.

Divorce: None.

PROBATE LAWS

In General: M.C. §91-1-1.

Elective Share: ½ to all. M.C. §§91-1-7; 91-5-25; 91-5-27.

Intestate Share: Equal portion with children, to all. M.C. §91-1-7.

DIVORCE LAWS

Title of Divorce Action: Divorce.

Property: There are no statutory provisions for property division, which leaves the matter up to the judge interpreting prior appellate court decisions. These are mostly based on the concept of "title," in which each party keeps what is titled in his or her name. Jointly titled property will be divided by the judge. This system has a history of favoring the husband. Judges have offset an otherwise unfair result by liberally awarding lump-sum alimony, or by considering the wife's contributions to acquiring the property.

Alimony: There are no statutory factors. Either party may be awarded alimony. Fault not considered. See M.C. §93-5-23.

MISSOURI

THE LAW

In General: *Vernon's* Annotated Missouri Statutes, Chapter 474, Section 474.120 (A.M.S. §474.120). [Look for volume 24.]

UPAA: No.

Probate: Waiver provided for in A.M.S. §474.220. A.M.S. §474.120). Similar to standard UPC waiver provision.

Divorce: A.M.S. §§451.220 to 451.240. Agreement must be in writing and acknowledged or proved by at least one witness.

PROBATE LAWS

In General: A.M.S. §474.010. [Look for volume 26.]

Elective share: ¹/₃ to ¹/₂. A.M.S. §474.160.

Intestate Share: ¹/₂ to all. A.M.S. §474.010.

DIVORCE LAWS

Title of Divorce Action: Dissolution of Marriage.

Property: Equitable distribution. Nonmarital property is property: (1) acquired before marriage; (2) acquired by gift or inheritance; (3) acquired in exchange for (1) or (2); (4) acquired after a decree of legal separation; (5) designated by agreement; or (6) increased in value, except due to marital labor or assets. Factors for dividing marital property: (1) economic circumstances of the parties, including whether custodian should remain in marital home; (2) each party's contribution to acquisition of property; (3) value of nonmarital property; (4) each party's conduct during marriage; (5) custody arrangements; and (6) any other relevant factor. A.M.S. §452.330.

Alimony: Called *maintenance*. Either party may be awarded if he or she: (1) lacks sufficient property to meet own needs; and (2) is unable to be self-supporting through appropriate employment. Amount and duration determined by: (1) financial resources of party seeking alimony; (2) time needed for education and training to obtain appropriate employment; (3) parties' comparative earning capacities; (4) standard of living established during marriage; (5) each party's obligations and assets; (6) duration of marriage; (7) age, physical and emotional condition of party seeking alimony; (8) ability of other party to meet own expenses while paying alimony; (9) each party's conduct during the marriage; and (10) any other relevant factor. Decree must state whether alimony may be modified. A.M.S. §452.335.

MONTANA

The Law

In General: Montana Code Annotated 1997, Title 40, Chapter 2, Section 40-2-601 (M.C.A. §40-2-601). The Montana Code Annotated is a set of black, soft-cover volumes. The annotations are in a separate set of loose-leaf binders.

UPAA: M.C.A. §40-2-601. [Look for volume 7.]

Probate: M.C.A. §72-2-102. Standard UPC waiver provision.

Divorce: None.

Probate Laws

In General: UPC: M.C.A. §72-1-101. [Look for volume 9.]

Elective Share: 3% to 50%, based on length of marriage. M.C.A. §72-2-221.

Intestate Share: ⅓ to all. M.C.A. §72-2-201.

Divorce Laws

Title of Divorce Action: Dissolution of Marriage.

Property: Equitable distribution. All property is marital property. Factors: (1) duration of the marriage, and any prior marriages; (2) each party's age, health, station, occupation, amount and sources of income, vocational skills, employability, estate, liabilities, and needs; (3) child custody provisions; (4) whether property division is in lieu of or in addition to alimony; (5) each party's opportunity for future acquisition of capital assets and income; and (6) each party's contribution to or dissipation of the value of property. If property was acquired prior to marriage, by gift or inheritance, in exchange for such property, or increased value of such property, or acquired after a decree of legal separation, the following factors are considered: (1) any nonmonetary contributions of a homemaker; (2) the extent such contribution facilitated maintenance of the property; and (3) whether property division is an alternative to alimony. M.C.A. §40-4-202.

Alimony: Called *maintenance*. Fault not considered. Either party may be awarded alimony if he or she: (1) lacks sufficient property to meet own needs; and (2) is unable to be self-supporting through appropriate employment. Amount and duration determined by: (1) financial resources of the party seeking alimony; (2) time needed for education and training to obtain appropriate employment; (3) standard of living established during marriage; (4) duration of the marriage; (5) age, physical and emotional condition of the party seeking alimony; and (6) the other party's ability to meet own expenses while paying alimony. M.C.A. §40-4-203.

NEBRASKA

THE LAW

In General: Revised Statutes of Nebraska, Chapter 42, Article 2, Section 42-205 (R.S.N. §42-205).

UPAA: No.

Probate: R.S.N. §30-2316. Standard UPC waiver provision.

Divorce: R.S.N. §42-205, which provides: "Nothing contained in section 42-201 to 42-205 shall invalidate any marriage settlement or contract."

PROBATE LAWS

In General: UPC: R.S.N. §30-2201 [Nebraska Probate Code.]

Elective Share: ¹/₂. R.S.N. §30-2313.

Intestate Share: ¹/₂ to all. R.S.N. §30-2302. Also provides for homestead (R.S.N. §30-2322); exempt property (R.S.N. §30-2323); and family allowance (R.S.N. §30-2324).

DIVORCE LAWS

Title of Divorce Action: Dissolution of Marriage.

Property: Equitable distribution. All property is marital, although fact that property was acquired before marriage, or by gift or inheritance, is considered as part of the circumstances of the parties. Case of *Lord v. Lord*, 213 Neb. 557, 330 N.W.2d 492 (1983). Factors: (1) circumstances of the parties; (2) duration of the marriage; (3) each party's contributions to the marriage, including the care and education of the children and any interruption of personal careers or educational opportunities; and (4) the ability of the party seeking alimony to engage in gainful employment without interfering with the interests of a child in that party's custody. R.S.N. §42-365.

Alimony: Fault not considered. Factors: (1) circumstances of the parties; (2) duration of the marriage; (3) each party's contributions to the marriage, including the care and education of the children and any interruption of personal careers or educational opportunities; and (4) the ability of the party seeking alimony to engage in gainful employment without interfering with the interests of a child in that party's custody. R.S.N. §42-365.

NEVADA

THE LAW

In General: Nevada Revised Statutes Annotated, Chapter 123A, Section 123A.010 (N.R.S.A. §123A.010).

UPAA: N.R.S.A. §123A.010.

Probate: None.

Divorce: None.

PROBATE LAWS

In General: N.R.S.A. §132.010.

Elective Share: Homestead allowance and "reasonable support." R.S.A. §146.010.

Intestate Share: ⅓ to all. N.R.S.A. §§134.040 and 134.050.

DIVORCE LAWS

Title of Divorce Action: Divorce.

Property: Community property. Separate property is property: (1) acquired before marriage; (2) acquired by gift or inheritance; (3) income or profits from (1) and (2); (4) designated separate by written agreement; (5) acquired after a decree of separate maintenance; and (6) acquired as personal injury damages. N.R.S.A. §§125.130 and 125.220. Marital property divided "...as appears just and equitable, having regard to the respective merits of the parties and to the condition in which they will be left by the divorce" and giving consideration "...to the party through whom the property was acquired, and to the burdens, if any, imposed upon it, for the benefit of the children." N.R.S.A. §125.150.

Alimony: Fault not considered. May be granted to either party "...as appears just and equitable, having regard to the respective merits of the parties and to the condition in which they will be left by the divorce." Alimony for training or education may be awarded upon consideration of: (1) whether the party to pay alimony has obtained greater job skills or education during the marriage; and (2) whether the party seeking alimony provided financial support while the other party obtained job skills or education. If ordered, the decree must state the time within which the training or education must begin. N.R.S.A. §125.150.

NEW HAMPSHIRE

THE LAW

In General: New Hampshire Revised Statutes Annotated, Chapter 560, Section 560:14 (N.H.R.S.A. §560:14). [Look for volume 5.]

UPAA: No.

Probate: N.H.R.S.A. §§560:14; 560:15; and 560:16. These sections only provide for waiver of the elective share, and that any agreement between the spouses is to be enforced by the probate court.

Divorce: None.

PROBATE LAWS

In General: N.H.R.S.A. §560:1 through 563-A:4.

Elective Share: ⅓ or more depending upon various circumstances. N.H.R.S.A. §560:10.

Intestate Share: ½ to all. N.H.R.S.A. §561:1.

DIVORCE LAWS

Title of Divorce Action: Divorce.

Property: Equitable distribution. Fault is a factor. Separate property is property acquired (1) before marriage or in exchange for such property; and (2) by gift or inheritance. Equal division of marital property, unless inequal division is justified considering: (1) duration of the marriage; (2) age, health, social or economic status, occupation, vocational skills, employability, separate property, amount and sources of income, needs and liabilities of the parties; (3) each party's opportunity for future acquisition of capital assets and income; (4) ability of custodial parent to engage in gainful employment without substantially interfering with the interests of the child; (5) custodial parent's need to remain in the marital home; (6) action during the marriage which contributed to the growth or diminution in value of any property; (7) any significant disparity between the parties in relation to contribution to the marriage; (8) any contribution to help educate or develop the career or employability of the other, and any interruption in one party's education or career opportunities for the benefit of the other's career, the marriage, or the children; (9) any expectation of pension or retirement rights acquired prior to or during the marriage; (10) tax consequences; (12) either party's fault for the breakdown of the marriage if fault was the cause and either (a) it caused substantial physical or mental pain and suffering, or (b) it resulted in substantial economic loss to the marital estate or to the injured party; (13) value of each parties' separate property; and (14) any other relevant factor. If division is not equal, the reasons must be stated in the decree. N.H.R.S.A. §458:19. See N.H.R.S.A. §458:7 for fault.

Alimony: Either party may be awarded if that party: (1) lacks income or property to maintain a standard of living similar to that during the marriage; and (2) is unable to support self through employment, or has child custody duties making it inadvisable to be employed; and (3) the party to pay has the ability to pay and meet his or her own needs. Amount and duration of alimony to be determined considering: (1) length of marriage; (2) age, health, social or economic status, occupation, amount and sources of income, property awarded, vocational skills, employability, estate, liabilities, and needs of each party; (3) each party's opportunity for future acquisition of capital assets and income; (4) fault; (5) federal tax consequences; (6) each party's contribution to the acquisition, preservation or appreciation in value of assets and to the family unit. The decree must state the reasons for granting or denying alimony. N.H.R.S.A. §458:193

NEW JERSEY

THE LAW

In General: NJSA (for New Jersey Statutes Annotated), Title 37, Chapter 2, Section 37:2-31 (N.J.S.A. §37:2-31).

UPAA: N.J.S.A. §37:2-31.

Probate: N.J.S.A. §3B:8-10. Standard UPC-type waiver provision.

Divorce: None.

PROBATE LAWS

In General: N.J.S.A. §3B:1-1.

Elective Share: ¹/₃. N.J.S.A. §3B:8-1.

Intestate Share: ¹/₂ to all. N.J.S.A. §3B:5-3.

DIVORCE LAWS

Title of Divorce Action: Divorce.

Property: Equitable distribution. Each party keeps property acquired before marriage or by gift or inheritance. Factors: (1) duration of marriage; (2) age, physical and emotional condition of parties; (3) property or income prior to marriage; (4) standard of living established during marriage; (5) any written agreement as to property division; (6) economic circumstances of each; (7) income and earning capacity of each; (8) contribution to the other party's education, training or earning power; (9) contribution to acquisition, dissipation, preservation, depreciation or appreciation of marital property; (10) tax consequences; (11) present value of property; (12) need of custodial parent to remain in the marital home; (13) debts and liabilities of each; (14) need for trust fund to secure foreseeable medical or educational costs for a child or spouse; (15) any other relevant factor. N.J.S.A. §2A:34-23.1.

Alimony: Fault not considered. Factors: (1) actual need and ability of parties to pay; (2) duration of the marriage; and age, physical and emotional condition of the parties; (4) standard of living established during the marriage, and the likelihood each can maintain that standard; (5) earning capacity, educational level, vocational skills and employability of the parties; (6) length of absence from the job market and child custodial responsibilities of the party seeking alimony; (7) time and expense needed for education and training; availability of training and employment; and the opportunity for future acquisition of capital assets and income; (8) contribution of each to the marriage; (9) property division; and (10) any other relevant factor. N.J.S.A. §2A:34-23.

NEW MEXICO

The Law

In General: New Mexico Statutes 1978 Annotated, Chapter 40, Section 40-2-1 (N.M.S.A. §40-2-1). Supplement is found at the end of each chapter.

UPAA: No.

Probate: None.

Divorce: N.M.S.A. §§40-2-1 to 40-2-9). Section 40-2-4 provides: "All contracts for marriage settlements and contracts for separation, must be in writing, and executed and acknowledged or proved in like manner as a grant of land is required to be executed and acknowledged or proved."

Probate Laws

In General: UPC: N.M.S.A. §45-1-101 [Probate Code.]

Elective Share: No statutory provision for elective share, but surviving spouse gets $^1/_2$ of the community property estate.

Intestate Share: $^1/_4$ to all. N.M.S.A. §45-2-102. There is also a family allowance of 10,000 and a personal property allowance of $3,500.

Divorce Laws

Title of Divorce Action: Dissolution of Marriage.

Property: Community property. Separate property is property: (1) acquired before marriage; (2) acquired after a decree of legal separation; (3) designated separate by court order or written agreement of the parties; or (4) acquired by gift or inheritance. N.M.S.A. §40-3-8. Fault not considered. No statutory factors. N.M.S.A. §40-4-7.

Alimony: Fault not considered. Alimony may be awarded to either party "as under the circumstances of the case may seem just and property. N.M.S.A. §40-4-7.

NEW YORK

THE LAW

In General: *McKinney's* Consolidated Laws of New York Annotated, General Obligations, Section 3-303 (C.L.N.Y., Gen.O. §3-303). New York's laws are divided into subjects, so be sure you have the correctly titled volume. or premarital agreement forms specifically for New York, see a separate set of books called West's McKinney's Forms, §§4:13 to 4:19A.

UPAA: No.

Misc: C.L.N.Y., General Obligations §3-303, which provides: "A contract made between persons in contemplation of marriage, remains in full force after the marriage takes place." [Look for volume 23A, titled "General Obligations."]

Probate: C.L.N.Y., Estates, Powers and Trusts Law §5-1.3, which makes reference to "ante nuptial agreement" as it relates to a waiver of the elective share when the deceased person's will pre-dates the marriage.

Divorce: None.

PROBATE LAWS

In General: C.L.N.Y., 4 volumes designated 17B, titled "Estates, Powers and Trusts Law," and volume 58A, titled "Surrogate's Court Procedure Act."

Elective Share: $^1/_3$ to $^1/_2$, although this is a lengthy section which needs to be fully considered. C.L.N.Y., Estates, Powers and Trusts Law §5-1.1.

Intestate Share: $4,000 plus $^1/_2$ residue, to all. C.L.N.Y., Estates, Powers & Trusts Law §4-1.1.

DIVORCE LAWS

Title of Divorce Action: Divorce.

Property: Equitable distribution. Separate property is: (1) property acquired before marriage; (2) property acquired by gift or inheritance; (3) compensation for personal injuries; (4) property acquired in exchange for, or increase in value of, (1) or (2), unless due to the efforts of the other party; and (5) property designated as separate in a written agreement of the parties. Marital property is divided according to the following factors: (1) income and property at time of marriage and at the commencement of the divorce; (2) duration of marriage, and age and health of the parties; (3) need of party with child custody to remain in the marital home; (4) loss of inheritance or pension rights; (5) alimony award, if any; (6) contribution of each to the acquisition of the property; (7) liquidity of the marital property; (8) probable future financial circumstances of each party; (9) difficulty in evaluating an asset or business entity; (10) tax consequences; (11) either party's wasteful dissipation of assets; (12) any transfer or encumbrance in contemplation of divorce without fair consideration; and (13) any other relevant factor. C.L.N.Y., Domestic Relations Law §236-Part B.

Alimony: Fault not considered. Factors: (1) income and property distribution; (2) duration of marriage, and the age and health of the parties; (3) present and future earning capacity of each; (4) ability of the party seeking alimony to become self-supporting, and the training and time needed; (5) the reduced earning capacity due to career building of the other party; (6) child custody arrangement; (7) tax consequences; (8) contribution to the career of the other party; (9) either party's wasteful dissipation of marital property; (10) any transfer or encumbrance in contemplation of divorce without fair consideration; and (11) any other relevant factor. C.L.N.Y., Domestic Relations Law §236-Part B.

NORTH CAROLINA

The Law

In General: General Statutes of North Carolina, Chapter 52B, Section 52B-1 (G.S.N.C. §52B-1).

UPAA: G.S.N.C. §52B-1). [Look for volume 8.]

Probate: None.

Divorce: None.

Probate Laws

In General: G.S.N.C, Chapters 28A through 31C. [Look for volume 7.]

Elective Share: ¹/₃ to all. G.S.N.C. §§29-14 and 30-1.

Intestate Share: ¹/₃ to all. G.S.N.C. §29-14.

Divorce Laws

Title of Divorce Action: Divorce.

Property: Equitable distribution. Fault not considered. Separate property is property: (1) acquired before marriage or by gift or inheritance; (2) acquired in exchange for such property; (3) any increase in value of, or income from, separate property; (4) non-transferable professional or business licenses; and (5) any non-vested retirement benefits. Division of marital property is to be equal, unless the judge decides this would not be equitable, considering: (1) income, property and liabilities of each party; (2) any obligation of support from a prior marriage; (3) duration of the marriage, and the age, physical and mental health of the parties; (4) need of the child custodian to occupy the marital home; (5) any expectation of non-vested retirement benefits; (6) each party's contribution to the acquisition of property; (7) the contribution of either party to the other's education or career development; (8) any direct contribution to the increase in value of the other's separate property; (9) liquidity of marital assets; (10) difficulty in evaluating any assets or business interest, and the economic desirability of retaining such an asset or business interest free of the other's intervention; (11) tax consequences; and (12) acts of either party to maintain, preserve, develop, expand, waste, neglect, devalue, or convert marital property after separation; and any other relevant factor. G.S.N.C. §50-20.

Alimony: Alimony may be awarded if the party seeking it is a "dependent spouse," and the other party is at fault (use grounds for legal separation). G.S.N.C. §50-16.2. No alimony is allowed if the party seeking it is guilty of adultery, or if alimony is barred by a valid separation agreement. G.S.N.C. §50-16.6. If alimony is awarded, the amount and duration is determined by the following factors: the parties' "estates, earnings, earning capacity, condition, accustomed standard of living of the parties, and other facts of the particular case." G.S.N.C. §50-16.6.

NORTH DAKOTA

The Law

In General: North Dakota Century Code Annotated, Title 14, Chapter 14-03.1, Section 14-03.1-01 (N.D.C.C. §14-03.1-01).

UPAA: N.D.C.C. §14-03.1-01). [Look for volume 3A.]

Probate: None.

Divorce: None.

Probate Laws

Probate: UPC: N.D.C.C. §30.1-01-01.

Elective Share: $^{1}/_{3}$. N.D.C.C. §30.1-05-01. [Look for volume 6.]

Intestate Share: $^{1}/_{2}$ to all. N.D.C.C. §30.1-04-02.

Divorce Laws

Title of Divorce Action: Divorce.

Property: Equitable distribution. All property, regardless of how or when acquired (although this is a factor to be considered) will be divided as judge feels is just. No statutory factors. N.D.C.C. §14-05-24.

Alimony: Fault is a factor. No other statutory factors. N.D.C.C. §14-05-24.

OHIO

THE LAW

In General: Page's Ohio Revised Code Annotated, Title 31, Section 3103.05 (O.R.C §3103.05). [Look for volume marked "Title 31." The first two numbers in the section number indicate the "Title" number.]

UPAA: No.

Misc: Page's Ohio Revised Code Annotated, Section 3103.05 (O.R.C §3103.05), which provides: "A husband or wife may enter into any engagement or transaction with the other, or with any other person, which either might if unmarried; subject, in transactions between themselves, to the general rules which control the actions of persons occupying confidential relations with each other."

Probate: None.

Divorce: None.

PROBATE LAWS

In General: O.R.C. §2101.01 through 2107.77. [Look for volume marked "Title 21."]

Elective Share: ¹/₃ to ¹/₂. O.R.C. §2106.01 (1991 Supplement).

Intestate Share: $20,000 plus ¹/₃ residue, to all. O.R.C. §2105.06.

DIVORCE LAWS

Title of Divorce Action: Divorce (general procedure), or Dissolution of Marriage (simplified procedure if both parties sign petition and have settlement agreement).

Property: Equitable distribution. Separate property is property: (1) acquired prior to marriage; (2) acquired by inheritance; (3) passive income and appreciation of separate property; (4) acquired after a decree of legal separation; (5) excluded by an antenuptial agreement; (6) obtained as personal injury compensation; or (7) clearly acquired as a gift to only one party. Marital property is divided considering: (1) duration of the marriage; (2) assets and liabilities of each party; (3) desirability of child custodian remaining in the marital home; (4) economic desirability of retaining intact assets or business interests; (5) tax consequences; (6) costs of sale, if sale is necessary; (7) any division pursuant to a separation agreement; and (8) any other relevant factor. O.R.C. §§3105.171.

Alimony: Referred to as *spousal support*. Court will determine property division first. Fault not considered. Factors: (1) income; (2) earning ability; (3) age, physical, mental and emotional condition; (4) retirement benefits; (5) duration of the marriage; (6) extent it would be inappropriate for the party with child custody to seek outside employment; (7) standard of living established during the marriage; (8) education; (9) assets and liabilities; (10) one party's contribution to the other's education, training or earning ability; (11) the time and expense to obtain education and training; (12) tax consequences; (13) income loss due to marital responsibilities; and (14) any other relevant factor. O.R.C. §3105.18.

OKLAHOMA

The Law

In General: Oklahoma Statutes Annotated, Title 84, Section 44 (84 O.S.A. §44).

UPAA: No.

Probate: 84 O.S.A. §44, which provides: "Every estate in property may be disposed of by will except that a will shall be subservient to any antenuptial marriage contract in writing."

Divorce: None.

Probate Laws

In General: Title 84, O.S.A.

Elective share: ¹/₂. 84 O.S.A. §44.

Intestate Share: ¹/₃ to all. 84 O.S.A. §213.

Divorce Laws

Title of Divorce Action: Divorce.

Property: Equitable distribution. Separate property is property acquired (1) before marriage, or (2) after marriage "in his or her own right." Fault not considered. Marital property divided in a just and reasonable manner. O.S.A. §43-121.

Alimony: Fault not considered. No statutory factors. See O.S.A. §§43-121.

OREGON

THE LAW

In General: Oregon Revised Statutes Annotated, Chapter 108, Section 108.700 (O.R.S. §108.700).

UPAA: O.R.S. §108.700. [Look for volume 7.]

Probate: None.

Divorce: None.

PROBATE LAWS

In General: O.R.S., Chapters 111 through 119.

Elective Share: $1/2$. O.R.S. §112.735.

Intestate Share: $1/2$ to all. O.R.S.§§112.025 and 112.035.

DIVORCE LAWS

Title of Divorce Action: Dissolution of Marriage.

Property: Equitable distribution. Fault not considered. O.R.S. §107.036. All property is divided according to the following factors: (1) cost of any sale of assets; (2) taxes and liens on property; (3) each party's contribution to acquisition of the property, including as homemaker; (4) retirement or social security benefits; (5) life insurance; (6) relationship of property award to alimony. Presumption that both parties contributed equally to acquiring property. O.R.S. §107.105(1)(f).

Alimony: Called *support*. Fault not considered. O.R.S. §107.036. Party receiving alimony must make reasonable efforts to become self-supporting within 10 years, or alimony may be terminated. O.R.S. §107.412. Factors: (1) length of marriage; (2) age, physical and mental health of parties; (3) any contribution to the other's education, training, or earning power; (4) each party's earning capacity; (5) need for education, training or retraining for suitable employment; (6) extent to which earning capacity is impaired due to absence from the job market as a homemaker, job opportunity unavailability due to age, and length of time needed to obtain training or update job skills; (7) any custody responsibilities; (8) tax consequences; (9) amount of long-term financial obligations; (10) costs of health care; (11) standard of living established during the marriage; (12) any court-ordered life insurance to secure support; and (13) any other relevant factor. O.R.S. §107.105(1)(d).

PENNSYLVANIA

THE LAW

In General: *Purdon's* Pennsylvania Consolidated Statutes Annotated, Title 23, Section 3104 (23 Pa. C.S.A. §3104).

UPAA: No.

Probate: None.

Divorce: 23 Pa. C.S.A. §3104). This section gives the court jurisdiction to determine rights created by an antenuptial agreement.

PROBATE LAWS

In General: Title 20, Pa.C.S.A. [Title 20 is in four volumes.]

Elective share: $^1/_3$. 20 Pa.C.S.A. §2203.

Intestate Share: $^1/_2$ to all. 20 Pa.C.S.A. §2102.

DIVORCE LAWS

Title of Divorce Action: Divorce.

Property: Equitable distribution. Non-marital property includes property: (1) acquired before marriage, by gift or inheritance; (2) acquired after separation, unless in exchange for marital property; (3) designated non-marital in a valid agreement; (4) sold or mortgaged in good faith and for value before separation; (5) acquired in payment of an award or settlement for a claim accrued prior to the marriage or after separation; or (6) certain veterans benefits. 23 Pa.C.S.A. §3501. Marital property is divided considering: (1) length of marriage; (2) any prior marriages of the parties; (3) age, health, station, amount and sources of income, vocational skills, employability, estate, liabilities and needs of each party; (4) contribution to the education, training or increased earning power of the other; (5) opportunity of each for future acquisition of capital assets or income; (6) each party's sources of income, including medical, retirement and insurance benefits; (7) each party's contribution or dissipation to the acquisition, preservation, depreciation or appreciation of marital property; (8) value of separate property; (9) standard of living established during the marriage; (10) economic circumstances of the parties, including tax consequences; and (11) whether either party will be custodian of any children. 23 Pa.C.S.A. §3502(a).

Alimony: Factors: (1) relative earnings and earning capacities of the parties; (2) ages, physical, mental and emotional condition of the parties; (3) sources of income, including medical, retirement and insurance benefits; (4) "expectations and inheritances"; (5) duration of the marriage; (6) contribution to the education, training or increased earning power of the other party; (7) extent to which the earning power, expenses or financial obligations are affected by serving as child custodian; (8) standard of living established during the marriage; (9) the parties' relative education, and time needed to acquire education and training to become adequately employed; (10) relative assets and liabilities; (11) property brought to the marriage; (12) contribution of a spouse as homemaker; (13) the parties' relative needs; (14) any marital misconduct during the marriage, up to separation; (15) tax ramifications; (16) whether the party seeking alimony lacks sufficient property to provide for his or her needs; and (17) whether the party seeking alimony is incapable of self-support through employment. 23 Pa.C.S.A. §3701. Cohabitation with a non-relative member of the opposite sex terminates alimony. 23 Pa.C.S.A. §3706.

RHODE ISLAND

THE LAW

In General: General Laws of Rhode Island, Section 15-17-1 (G.L.R.I. §15-17-1). Ignore "Title" and "Chapter" numbers.

UPAA: G.L.R.I. §15-17-1. [Look for volume 3A.]

Probate: None.

Divorce: None.

PROBATE LAWS

In General: G.L.R.I. §33-1-1. [Look for volume 6.]

Elective Share: Life estate in the real property. G.L.R.I. §§33-1-5, 33-25-2, and 33-25-4. Court may also give up to $25,000 in real estate. G.L.R.I. §33-1-6.

Intestate Share: Life estate in real property. G.L.R.I. §33-1-5. At court's discretion, up to $75,000 in real property. G.L.R.I. §33-1-6.

DIVORCE LAWS

Title of Divorce Action: Divorce.

Property: Equitable distribution. Separate property is property acquired before marriage or by gift or inheritance. Factors for dividing marital property: (1) length of the marriage; (2) conduct of parties during marriage; and (3) each party's contribution to the acquisition, preservation or appreciation in value of the asset, including as homemaker. G.L.R.I. §15-5-16.1.

Alimony: Factors: (1) length of marriage; (2) conduct during marriage; (3) each party's health, age, station, occupation, amount and sources of income, vocational skills, and employability; and (4) each party's "state" [probably intended to be "estate"], liabilities and needs. G.L.R.I. §15-5-16.

SOUTH CAROLINA

THE LAW

In General: Code of Laws of South Carolina, Title 20, Section 20-5-50 (C.L.S.C. §20-5-50). [Look for volume 8], which provides: "All marriage contracts, deeds and settlements shall therein describe, specify and particularize the real and personal estate thereby intended to be included, comprehended, conveyed and passed or shall have a schedule thereto annexed containing a description and the particulars and articles of the real and personal estate intended to be conveyed and passed by such marriage contracts, deeds and settlements. Any such schedule shall be annexed to the contract, deed or other settlement paper, signed, executed and delivered by the parties therein interested at the time of the signing, executing and delivering the marriage contract, deed or settlement, be subscribed by the same witness who subscribed the marriage contract, deed or settlement and be recorded therewith; otherwise, and in default of such schedule and recording thereof as aforesaid, the marriage contract, deed or settlement shall be deemed and declared to be fraudulent, null and void with respect to and against creditors and bona fide purchasers or mortgagees."

UPAA; Probate and Divorce: None.

PROBATE LAWS

In General: UPC: C.L.S.C. §62-1-100 (Referred to as the South Carolina Probate Code.) [Look for volume 20B.]

Elective share: ⅓. C.L.S.C. §62-2-201. Intestate share is ½ to all. C.L.S.C. §62-2-102.

Intestate Share: ½ to all. C.L.S.C. §62-2-102.

DIVORCE LAWS

Title of Divorce Action: Divorce.

Property: Equitable distribution. Nonmarital property is property: (1) acquired before marriage; (2) acquired by gift or inheritance; (3) acquired after an order in a divorce or separate maintenance action; (4) acquired after signing a settlement agreement; (5) acquired after a permanent court order regarding property; (6) acquired in exchange for any of the above property; (7) designated as such in a written agreement of the parties; and (8) any increase in value of any such property, unless due to the other's efforts. The court has no jurisdiction to award one party the other's nonmarital property. C.L.S.C. §20-7-473. Marital property divided considering: (1) duration of marriage, and the parties' ages at the time of marriage and now; (2) any marital misconduct or fault; (3) value of marital property, and each party's contribution to the acquisition, preservation, depreciation or appreciation of assets; (4) each party's income, earning potential and opportunity for future acquisition of capital assets; (5) each party's physical and emotional health; (6) each party's need for training or education; (7) each party's nonmarital property; (8) existence of any vested retirement benefits; (9) whether alimony was awarded; (10) whether the custodial party should remain in the marital home; (11) tax consequences; (12) any other support obligations; (13) any encumbrances on property, and other debt; (14) any child custody arrangements and obligations; and (15) any other relevant factor. C.L.S.C. §20-7-472.

Alimony: Either party may be awarded alimony. Factors: (1) duration of marriage, and the parties' ages at the time of marriage and now; (2) each party's physical and emotional condition; (3) educational background, and need for additional training or education; (4) employment history and earning potential; (5) standard of living established during marriage; (6) current and reasonably anticipated earnings; (7) current and reasonably anticipated expenses and needs; (8) all property; (9) any child custody conditions and circumstances; (10) any marital misconduct or fault; (11) tax consequences; (12) any other support obligations; and (13) any other relevant factor. C.L.S.C. §20-3-120.

SOUTH DAKOTA

THE LAW

In General: South Dakota Codified Laws, Title 25, Chapter 2, Section 25-2-16 (S.D.C.L. §25-2-16).

UPAA: S.D.C.L. §25-2-16. [Look for volume 9A.]

Probate: S.D.C.L. §30-5A-4. Standard UPC-type waiver provision.

Divorce: None.

PROBATE LAWS

In General: S.D.C.L. §29-1-1. [Look for volume 9B.]

Elective Share: Up to ⅓, or $100,000, whichever is greater. S.D.C.L. §30-5A-5.

Intestate Share: ⅓ to all. S.D.C.L. §§29-1-5 and 29-1-6.

DIVORCE LAWS

Title of Divorce Action: Divorce.

Property: Equitable distribution. No separate property mentioned in the Code. Fault not considered. S.D.C.L. §25-4-45.1. Only factor is statute is the circumstances of the parties, which courts have interpreted by using the usual factors, including the value of each party's property. See S.D.C.L. §25-4-44.

Alimony: Only factor in statute is the "equity and circumstances of the parties." Fault is considered. S.D.C.L. §25-4-41.

TENNESSEE

THE LAW

In General: Tennessee Code Annotated, Title 66, Section 66-24-105 (T.C.A. §66-24-105). Refers to registration requirements for protection against creditors. [Look for volume 11A.]

UPAA: No.

Probate: None.

Divorce: T.C.A. §36-3-501 [Look for volume 6A], which provides: "Notwithstanding any other provision of law to the contrary, except as provided in §36-3-502, any antenuptial or prenuptial agreement entered into by spouses concerning property owned by either spouse before the marriage which is the subject of such agreement shall be binding upon any court having jurisdiction over such spouses and/or such agreement if such agreement is determined in the discretion of such court to have been entered into by such spouses freely, knowledgeably and in good faith and without exertion of duress or undue influence upon either spouse. The terms of such agreement shall be enforceable by all remedies available for enforcement of contract terms."

PROBATE LAWS

In General: T.C.A. §§30-1-101 to 32-5-110. [Look for volume 6.]

Elective Share: ⅓. T.C.A. §31-4-101.

Intestate Share: ⅓ to all. T.C.A. §31-2-104.

DIVORCE LAWS

Title of Divorce Action: Divorce.

Property: Equitable distribution. Separate property is property acquired (1) before marriage; (2) in exchange for such property; (3) as income or appreciation from such property; and (4) by gift or inheritance. Marital property divided according to following factors: (1) duration of the marriage; (2) each party's age, physical and mental health, vocational skills, employability, earning capacity, estate, financial liabilities and needs; (3) either party's tangible and intangible contribution to the education, training or increased earning power of the other; (4) the parties' relative abilities for future acquisition of capital assets and income; (5) each party's contribution to the acquisition, preservation, appreciation or dissipation of marital or separate property; (6) value of separate property; (7) estate of each at time of marriage; (8) economic circumstances at the time of property division; (9) tax consequences; and (10) any other relevant factor. T.C.A. §36-4-121.

Alimony: Factors: (1) Relative earning capacity, obligations, needs and financial resources; (2) relative education and training, and opportunity to secure education and training, and necessity to secure education and training, to improve earning capacity; (3) duration of the marriage; (4) age, physical and mental condition of each party; (5) any limitation on a party's earning capacity due to child custody responsibilities; (6) separate assets; (7) property division; (8) standard of living established during the marriage; (9) contribution to the marriage, and to the other's education, training and increased earning power; (10) relative fault of the parties; and (11) any other relevant factor, including tax consequences. T.C.A. §36-5-101.

TEXAS

THE LAW

In General: *Vernon's* Texas Codes Annotated, Family Code, Section 5.41 (T.C.A., Family Code §5.41). The Texas laws are divided into subjects, so be sure you have the volumes marked for the correct subject, such as "Family," or "Probate Code."

UPAA: T.C.A., Family Code §5.41. Be sure you have the volumes titled "Family."

Probate: None.

Divorce: None.

PROBATE LAWS

In General: Vernon's Texas Civil Statutes, Probate Code (referred to as "Texas Probate Code."). Again, be sure you have the volumes titled "Probate."

Elective Share: There is no specific statute for an elective share, but the surviving spouse is entitled to ½ of the community property estate. There is also a homestead allowance, family allowance, and exempt property. T.C.S., Probate Code §284.

Intestate Share: (a) ⅓ of the personal property and a life estate in ⅓ of the real property if there are children, and (b) all of the personal property and ½ of the real property if there are no children but there are parents or siblings of the deceased spouse (all of the real estate if no parents or siblings). T.C.S., Probate Code §38(b).

DIVORCE LAWS

Title of Divorce Action: Divorce.

Property: Community property. Separate property is that acquired prior to marriage, by gift or inheritance, or as personal injury recovery. Marital property divided equally, unless court finds this unjust. T.C.A., Family Code §§3.63, 3.632, 3.633 & 5.01.

Alimony: Alimony is not permitted after divorce; only until the final decree of divorce. T.C.A., Family Code §§3.58 & 3.59.

UTAH

THE LAW

In General: Utah Code Annotated 1953, Title 30, Section 30-2-1 (U.C.A. §30-2-1).

UPAA: No.

Probate: U.C.A. §75-2-204). [Look for volume 8A.] Standard UPC waiver provision.

Divorce: U.C.A. §§30-2-1 to 30-2-6. [Look for volume 3B.] These sections provide:
§30-2-1. Provides that the wife's property before marriage, or acquired during marriage as her separate property remains her property.
§30-2-2. "Contracts may be made by a wife, and liabilities incurred and enforced by or against her, to the same extent and in the same manner as if she were unmarried."
§30-2-3. "A conveyance, transfer or lien executed by either husband or wife to or in favor of the other shall be valid to the same extent as between other persons."
§30-2-6. "Should the husband or wife obtain possession or control of property belonging to the other before or after marriage, the owner of the property may maintain an action therefor, or for any right growing out of the same, in the same manner and to the same extent as if they were unmarried."

PROBATE LAWS

In General: UPC: U.C.A. §75-1-101. [Look for volume 8A.]

Elective Share: $1/3$. U.C.A. §75-2-201.

Intestate Share: $1/2$ to all. U.C.A. §75-2-102.

DIVORCE LAWS

Title of Divorce Action: Divorce.

Property: Equitable distribution. All property divided equitably, regardless of how or when acquired. No statutory factors. See U.C. §§30-3-5.

Alimony: No statutory factors. Fault not considered. See U.C. §30-3-5.

VERMONT

THE LAW

In General: Vermont Statutes Annotated, Title 14, Section 465 (14 V.S.A. §465). Ignore "Chapter" numbers.

UPAA: No.

Probate: Vermont Statutes Annotated, Title 14, Section 465 (14 V.S.A. §465). This law provides, in part: "If the widow was not the first wife of the deceased and he leaves no issue by her, and an agreement was entered into between them, previous to or after their marriage, in relation to the widow's claim on the estate of her husband in lieu of such third interest, and if, in the opinion of the court, she has a sufficient provision for her comfortable support during life, the court may deny to such widow such third part of his real estate or any provision other than such as is provided by the agreement of the parties."

Divorce: None.

PROBATE LAWS

In General: 14 V.S.A. §1.

Elective Share: ¹/₃ or more. 14 V.S.A. §§401 and 402.

Intestate Share: Minimum of ¹/₃ of personal property. 14 V.S.A. §401. Household goods. 14 V.S.A. §403. Reasonable support. 14 V.S.A. §404. ¹/₃ to ¹/₂ real property. 14.V.S.A. §§461 and 474.

DIVORCE LAWS

Title of Divorce Action: Divorce.

Property: Equitable distribution. All property divided regardless of how or when acquired, but how and by whom acquired is a factor. Concept of "separate property" is recognized, but not defined in statute. Factors: (1) length of marriage; (2) age and health of parties; (3) each party's occupation, and sources and amount of income; (4) each party's vocational skills and employability; (5) either party's contribution to the education, training and increased earning power of the other; (6) value of property, liabilities, and needs of each; (7) whether property division is in lieu of or in addition to alimony; (8) each party's opportunity for future acquisition of capital assets or income; (9) desirability of the custodial parent remaining in the marital home; (10) the party through whom the property was acquired; (11) each party's contribution to the acquisition, preservation, depreciation and appreciation of the property; and (12) the "respective merits of the parties." 15 V.S.A. §751.

Alimony: Fault not considered. May be awarded if (1) party seeking alimony lacks sufficient income or property to provide for his or her reasonable needs; and (2) is unable to support self through appropriate employment at the same standard of living established during the marriage, or is custodian of a child. Factors in determining amount and duration: (1) financial resources of the party seeking alimony, the property apportioned to him or her, ability to meet his or her own needs, and the extent to which child support contains an amount for him or her as custodian; (2) time and expense needed to acquire education and training to find appropriate employment; (3) standard of living established during marriage; (4) duration of marriage; (5) age, and physical and emotional condition of the parties; (6) ability of the person to pay alimony to meet his or her own needs while paying; and (7) "inflation with relation to the cost of living." 15 V.S.A.§752.

VIRGINIA

THE LAW

In General: Code of Virginia 1950, Title 20, Section 20-147 (C.V. §20-147). Ignore "Chapter" numbers, and look for "Title" and "Section" numbers.

UPAA: C.V. §20-147). [Look for volume 4A.]

Probate: None.

Divorce: None.

PROBATE LAWS

In General: C.V. §64.1-1. [Look for volume 9A.]

Elective Share: ¹/₃ to ¹/₂. C.V. §64.1-16.

Intestate share: ¹/₃ to all. C.V. §64.1-1.

DIVORCE LAWS

Title of Divorce Action: Divorce.

Property: Equitable distribution. Separate property is property acquired (1) before marriage; (2) by gift or inheritance; (3) by exchange for separate property, provided it was always maintained as separate property; and (4) any income from, or increase in value of, such property, unless the income or increase was from the efforts of the spouse. Factors for dividing marital property: (1) each party's contribution to the well-being of the family; (2) each party's contribution to the acquisition and care and maintenance of marital property; (3) duration of marriage; (4) age, physical and mental condition of the parties; (5) circumstances and factors contributing to the divorce; (6) how and when property was acquired; (7) each party's debts and liabilities, and the basis for, and property securing, such debts and liabilities; (8) liquid or nonliquid character of all marital property; (9) tax consequences; and (10) any other relevant factor. C.V. §20-107.3.

Alimony: In deciding whether alimony is appropriate the judge is to consider the circumstances and factors contributing to the divorce (adultery of the party seeking alimony will generally preclude alimony). Factors in determining amount: (1) each party's earning capacity, obligations, needs and financial resources; (2) each party's education and training, and ability to secure education and training; (3) standard of living established during the marriage; (4) duration of marriage; (5) age, physical and mental condition of each party; (6) each party's contribution to the well-being of the family; (7) each party's property interests; (8) the marital property division; (9) tax consequences; and (10) any other relevant factor. C.V. §20-107.1.

WASHINGTON

THE LAW

In General: *West's* Revised Code of Washington Annotated, Title 26, Chapter 26.16, Section 26.16.120 (R.C.W.A. §26.16.120)

UPAA: No.

Probate: None.

Divorce: R.C.W.A. §26.16.120), which provides: "Nothing contained in any of the provisions of this chapter or in any law of this state, shall prevent the husband and wife from jointly entering into any agreement concerning the status or disposition of the whole or any portion of the community property, then owned by them or afterwards to be acquired, to take effect upon the death of either. But such agreement may be made at any time by the husband and wife by the execution of an instrument in writing under their hands and seals, and to be witnessed, acknowledged and certified in the same manner as deeds to real estate are required to be, under the laws of the state, and the same may at any time thereafter be altered or amended in the same manner: Provided, however, that such agreement shall not derogate from the right of creditors, nor be construed to curtail the powers of the superior court to set aside or cancel such agreement for fraud or under some other recognized head of equity jurisdiction, at the suit of either party."

PROBATE LAWS

In General: R.C.W.A. §11.02.001.

Elective Share: No specific provision for elective share, but surviving spouse gets ¹/₂ of the community property estate.

Intestate Share: All of the community property estate, and ¹/₂ of the separate property if there are children, ³/₄ if no children but there are parents or siblings, all if no children, parents or siblings. R.C.W.A. §11.04.015.

DIVORCE LAWS

Title of Divorce Action: Dissolution of Marriage.

Property: Community property. Separate property is property acquired before marriage, or by gift or inheritance, and any income or increase in value of such property. R.C.W.A. §§26.16.010 and 26.16.020. Factors in dividing marital property: (1) nature and extent of community property; (2) nature and extent of separate property; (3) duration of marriage; (4) each party's economic circumstances, including whether the custodial party should remain in the marital home; and (5) any other relevant factor. §26.09.080.

Alimony: Fault not considered. Factors: (1) financial resources of the party seeking alimony; (2) time needed to acquire education and training to find employment suitable to the party's skills, interests, life style, and other circumstances of the party seeking alimony; (3) standard of living established during the marriage; (4) duration of marriage; (5) age, physical and emotional condition, and the financial obligations of the party seeking alimony; and (6) the ability of the other party to meet his or her own needs while paying alimony. R.C.W.A. §26.09.090.

WEST VIRGINIA

THE LAW

In General: West Virginia Code, Chapter 48, Article 2, Section 48-2-1(b) [W.V.C. §48-2-1(b)].

UPAA: No.

Misc: W.V.C. §48-2-1(b)]. [Look for volume 14.]

Probate: W.V.C. §43-3-3a. Waiver of elective share.

Divorce: None.

PROBATE LAWS

In General: W.V.C. §41-1-1 to 4-8-10. [Look for volume 12.]

Elective Share: 3% to 50%, depending upon the length of the marriage (must read statute for details). W.V.C. §42-3-1.

Intestate Share: ¹/₂ to all. W.V.C. §42-1-3.

DIVORCE LAWS

Title of Divorce Action: Divorce.

Property: Equitable distribution. Separate property is property: (1) acquired before marriage; (2) acquired in exchange for such property; (3) designated separate by a written agreement; (4) acquired by gift or inheritance; (5) acquired after separation of the parties; and (6) increases in value of separate property not due to the efforts of the parties. Fault is not considered. Marital property to be divided equally, but this may be altered upon consideration of: (1) extent each party contributed to acquisition, preservation and maintenance, or increase in value of marital property; (2) extent each party expended efforts during the marriage which limited or decreased that party's income earning ability, or increased the other party's income earning ability; (3) conduct of either party which dissipated or depreciated value of marital property. W.V.C. §48-2-32.

Alimony: Fault is a factor. Alimony is barred if party requesting (1) was adulterous, (2) was convicted of a felony during the marriage, or (3) deserted or abandoned spouse for 6 months. Factors: (1) length of marriage; (2) period of time during marriage the parties actually lived together; (3) present income and recurring earnings; (4) income earning abilities of the parties; (5) property division, as it affects earnings, need for alimony or ability to pay alimony; (6) age, physical, mental and emotional condition of each; (7) educational qualifications of each; (8) Likelihood that party seeking alimony can substantially increase his or her income earning abilities within a reasonable time by acquiring additional education or training; (9) anticipated expense of obtaining education and training; (10) cost of educating minor children; (11) cost of providing health care to both parties and children; (12) tax consequences; (13) extent to which it would be inappropriate for custodial party to seek employment outside home; (14) financial needs of both parties; (15) legal obligations of each party to support self or any others; and (16) any other relevant factors. W.V.C. §48-2-16.

WISCONSIN

The Law

In General: *West's* Wisconsin Statutes Annotated, Section 851.001 (W.S.A. §851.001). Ignore "Chapter" numbers. There are no references to premarital agreements in the Wisconsin Statutes.

UPAA: None.

Probate: None.

Divorce: None.

Probate Laws

In General: W.S.A. §851.001.

Elective Share: ¹/₂, but be sure to read statute. W.S.A. §861.03. For elective share, homestead and other rights, see the chapter on "Family Rights," beginning at W.S.A. §861.01. There are also special provisions for the surviving spouse retaining the marital home. W.S.A. §852.09.

Intestate Share: ¹/₂ to all. W.S.A. §852.01.

Divorce Laws

Title of Divorce Action: Divorce.

Property: Community property. Separate property is property acquired: (1) before marriage; (2) by gift or inheritance; or (3) with funds obtained before marriage or by gift or inheritance. (However, these types of property may even be divided to prevent hardship to a party). Fault is not considered. Marital property divided considering: (1) length of marriage; (2) property brought to marriage by each; (3) whether one party has substantial assets not subject to division by the court; (4) contribution of each party to marriage; (5) age, physical and emotional health of each; (6) contribution of one party to the other's education, training or increased earning power; (7) earning capacity of each, custodial responsibilities, and time and expense needed to acquire education or training to become self-supporting at a standard of living reasonably comparable to that during marriage; (8) desirability of custodial party remaining in marital home; (9) amount and duration of alimony or family support, and whether property division is in lieu of such payments; (10) other economic circumstances of the parties; (11) tax consequences; (12) any written agreements; and (13) any other relevant factor. W.S.A. §§766.01 & 767.255.

Alimony: Called *maintenance*. Fault is not considered. Either party may be granted alimony after considering: (1) length of marriage; (2) age, physical and emotional health of the parties; (3) property division; (4) each party's educational level at the time of marriage and now; (5) earning capacity of party seeking alimony, including custodial responsibilities, and time and expense needed to acquire education or training to find appropriate employment; (6) feasibility that party seeking alimony can become self-supporting at a standard of living similar to that during marriage, and length of time needed; (7) tax consequences; (8) any agreement of the parties; (9) either party's contribution to the other's education, training, or increased earning capacity; and (10) any other relevant factor. W.S.A. §§767.26.

WYOMING

THE LAW

In General: Wyoming Statutes Annotated, Title 1, Chapter 23, Section 1-23-105 (W.S.A. §1-23-105).

UPAA: No.

Misc: W.S.A. §1-23-105 [Look for volume 2], which provides that a contract in consideration of marriage must be in writing.

Probate: W.S.A. §2-5-102. Standard UPC-type waiver provision.

Divorce: None.

PROBATE LAWS

In General: W.S.A. §2-1-101. [Look for volumes 2 and 2A.]

Elective Share: $^1/_4$ to $^1/_2$. W.S.A. §2-5-101.

Intestate Share: $^1/_2$ to all. W.S.A. §2-4-101.

DIVORCE LAWS

Title of Divorce Action: Divorce.

Property: Equitable distribution. All property is divided, regardless of how and when acquired, although this is a factor. Fault is a factor. Factors: (1) respective merits of the parties; (2) condition each party will be left in after divorce; (3) the party through whom the property was acquired; and (4) the burdens imposed on the property for the benefit of either party or their children. W.S.A. §20-2-114. [Look for volume 5A.]

Alimony: Either party may be awarded "…reasonable alimony out of the estate of the other having regard for the other's ability." No other statutory factors. Fault is not considered. W.S.A. §20-2-114.

Uniform Premarital Agreement Act

Section 1. DEFINITIONS

As used in this Act:

(1) "Premarital Agreement" means an agreement between prospective spouses made in contemplation of marriage and to be effective upon marriage.

(2) "Property" means an interest, present or future, legal or equitable, vested or contingent, in real or personal property, including income and earnings.

Section 2. FORMALITIES

A premarital agreement must be in writing and signed by both spouses. It is enforceable without consideration.

Section 3. CONTENT

(a) Parties to a premarital agreement may contract with respect to:

   (1) the rights and obligations of each of the parties in any of the property of either or both of them whenever and wherever acquired or located;

   (2) the right to buy, sell, use, transfer, exchange, abandon, lease, consume, expend, assign, create a security interest in, mortgage, encumber, dispose of, or otherwise manage and control property;

   (3) the disposition of property upon separation, marital dissolution, death, or the occurrence or nonoccurrence of any other event;

   (4) the modification or elimination of spousal support;

   (5) the making of a will, trust, or other arrangement to carry out the provisions of the agreement;

   (6) the ownership of rights in and disposition of the death benefit from a life insurance policy;

   (7) the choice of law governing the construction of the agreement; and

   (8) any other matter, including their personal rights and obligations, not in violation of public policy or a statute imposing a criminal penalty.

(b) The right of a child to support may not be adversely affected by a premarital agreement.

Section 4. EFFECT OF MARRIAGE

A premarital agreement becomes effective upon marriage.

Section 5. AMENDMENT, REVOCATION

After marriage, a premarital agreement may be amended or revoked only by a written agreement signed by the parties. The amended agreement or the revocation is enforceable without consideration.

Section 6. ENFORCEMENT

(a) A premarital agreement is not enforceable if the party against whom enforcement is sought proves that:

    (1) that party did not execute the agreement voluntarily; or

    (2) the agreement was unconscionable when it was executed and, before execution of the agreement, that party:

        (i) was not provided a fair and reasonable disclosure of the property or financial obligations of the other party;

        (ii) did not voluntarily and expressly waive, in writing, any right to disclosure of the property or financial obligations of the other party beyond the disclosure provided; and

        (iii) did not have, or reasonably could not have had, an adequate knowledge of the property or financial obligations of the other party.

(b) If a provision of a premarital agreement modifies or eliminates spousal support and that modification or elimination causes one party to the agreement to be eligible for support under a program of public assistance at the time of separation or marital dissolution, a court, notwithstanding the terms of the agreement, may require the other party to provide support to the extent necessary to avoid that eligibility.

(c) An issue of unconscionability of a premarital agreement shall be decided by the court as a matter of law.

Section 7. ENFORCEMENT: VOID MARRIAGE

If a marriage is determined to be void, an agreement that would otherwise have been a premarital agreement is enforceable to the extent necessary to avoid an inequitable result.

Section 8. LIMITATION OF ACTIONS

Any statute of limitations applicable to an action asserting a claim for relief under a premarital agreement is tolled during the marriage of the parties to the agreement. However, equitable defenses limiting the time for enforcement, including laches and estoppel, are available to either party.

Section 9. APPLICATION AND CONSTRUCTION

This Act shall be applied and construed to effectuate its general purpose to make uniform the law with respect to the subject of this Act among states enacting it.

Section 10. SHORT TITLE

This Act may be cited as the Uniform Premarital Agreement Act.

Section 11. SEVERABILITY

If any provision of this Act or its application to any person or circumstance is held invalid, the invalidity does not affect other provisions or applications of this Act which can be given effect without the invalid provision or application, and to this end the provisions of this Act are severable.

Section 12. TIME OF TAKING EFFECT

This Act takes effect _____ and applies to any premarital agreement executed on or after that date.

Appendix D
Forms

This appendix contains sample forms for your use in preparing your own premarital agreement. You will not need all of these forms, but will need to choose the forms best suited to your situation and what you want to accomplish. You may also modify these forms as needed to fit your circumstances.

Form 2, is not necessarily a form to be used "as is." This form enables you to choose from alternative provisions, and put together a premarital agreement suited to your specific situation. You can also use it "as is" by placing an "X" in the appropriate boxes.

The following forms are included in this appendix, and can be found on the pages listed:

Premarital Agreement

This Agreement is entered into on _____, _____, by and between _____ (hereafter referred to as the Husband), and _____ (hereafter referred to as the Wife), who agree that:

1.   MARRIAGE. The parties plan to marry each other, and intend to provide in this agreement for their property and other rights that may arise because of their contemplated marriage.

2.   PURPOSE OF AGREEMENT. Both parties currently own assets, and anticipate acquiring additional assets, which they wish to continue to control and they are executing this Agreement to fix and determine their respective rights and duties during the marriage, in the event of a divorce or dissolution of the marriage, or on the death of one of the parties.

3.   FINANCIAL DISCLOSURE. The parties have fully revealed to each other full financial information regarding their net worth, assets, holdings, income, and liabilities; not only by their discussions with each other, but also through copies of their current financial statements, copies of which are attached hereto as Exhibits A and Exhibit B. Both parties acknowledge that they have had sufficient time to review the other's financial statement, are familiar with and understand the other's financial statement, have had any questions satisfactorily answered, and are satisfied that full and complete financial disclosure has been made by the other.

4.   ADVICE OF COUNSEL. Each party has had legal and financial advice, or has the opportunity to consult independent legal and financial counsel, prior to executing this agreement. Either party's failure to so consult legal and financial counsel constitutes a waiver of such right. By signing this agreement, each party acknowledges that he or she understands the facts of this agreement, and is aware of his or her legal rights and obligations under this agreement or arising because of their contemplated marriage.

5.   CONSIDERATION. The parties acknowledge that each of them would not enter into the contemplated marriage except for the execution of this agreement in its present form.

6.   EFFECTIVE DATE. This Agreement shall become effective and binding upon the marriage of the parties. In the event the marriage does not take place, this agreement shall be null and void.

7.   DEFINITIONS. As used in this agreement, the following terms shall have the following meanings:
      (a)   "Joint Property" means property held and owned by the parties together. Such ownership shall be as tenants by the entirety in jurisdictions where such a tenancy is permitted. If such jurisdiction does not recognize or permit a tenancy by the entirety, then

ownership shall be as joint tenants with rights of survivorship. The intention of the parties is to hold joint property as tenants by the entirety whenever possible.

(b) "Joint Tenancy" means tenancy by the entirety in jurisdictions where such a tenancy is permitted, and joint tenancy with rights of survivorship if tenancy by the entirety is not recognized or permitted. The intention of the parties is to hold joint property as tenants by the entirety whenever possible.

8. **HUSBAND'S SEPARATE PROPERTY.** The Husband is the owner of certain property, which is set forth and described in Exhibit C attached hereto and made a part hereof, which he intends to keep as his nonmarital, separate, sole, and individual property. All income, rents, profits, interest, dividends, stock splits, gains, and appreciation in value, relating to any such separate property shall also be deemed separate property.

9. **WIFE'S SEPARATE PROPERTY.** The Wife is the owner of certain property, which is set forth and described in Exhibit D attached hereto and made a part hereof, which she intends to keep as her nonmarital, separate, sole, and individual property. All income, rents, profits, interest, dividends, stock splits, gains, and appreciation in value, relating to any such separate property shall also be deemed separate property.

10. **JOINT OR COMMUNITY PROPERTY.** The parties intend that certain property shall, from the beginning of the marriage, be marital, joint, or community property, which is set forth and described in Exhibit E attached hereto and made a part hereof.

11. **PROPERTY ACQUIRED DURING MARRIAGE.** The parties recognize that either or both of them may acquire property during the marriage. The parties agree that the manner in which such property is titled during the marriage shall control such property's ownership and distribution in the event of any divorce, dissolution of marriage, separation, or death of either party. Such property shall be held as provided in the instrument conveying or evidencing title to such property. If the instrument does not specify or if there is no instrument, the property shall be held as a tenancy by the entirety, or as a joint tenancy with rights of survivorship in the event tenancy by the entirety is not recognized by the court having jurisdiction over the distribution of such property. Any property acquired that does not normally have a title or ownership certificate shall be considered as joint property unless otherwise specified by the parties in writing. All wedding gifts shall be deemed joint property, unless specified as separate property in either Exhibit C or D.

12. **BANK ACCOUNTS.** Any funds deposited in either party's separate bank accounts shall be deemed that party's separate property. Any funds deposited in a bank account held by the parties jointly shall be deemed joint property.

13. **PAYMENT OF EXPENSES.** The parties agree that their expenses shall be paid as set forth in Exhibit F attached hereto and made a part hereof.

14. **DISPOSITION OF PROPERTY.** Each party retains the management and control of the property belonging to that party and may encumber, sell, or dispose of the property

without the consent of the other party. Each party shall execute any instrument necessary to effectuate this paragraph on the request of the other party. If a party does not join in or execute an instrument required by this paragraph, the other party may sue for specific performance or for damages, regardless of the doctrine of spousal immunity, and the defaulting party shall be responsible for the other party's costs, expenses and attorney's fees. This paragraph shall not require a party to execute a promissory note or other evidence of debt for the other party. If a party executes a promissory note or other evidence of debt for the other party, that other party shall indemnify the party executing the note or other evidence of debt from any claims or demands arising from the execution of the instrument. Execution of an instrument shall not give the executing party any right or interest in the property or the party requesting execution.

15. **PROPERTY DIVISION UPON DIVORCE, DISSOLUTION OF MARRIAGE, OR SEPARATION.** In the event of divorce, dissolution of marriage, or separation proceedings being filed and pursued by either party, the parties agree that the terms and provisions of this agreement shall govern all of their rights as to property, alimony including permanent periodic, rehabilitative, and lump sum, property settlement, rights of community property, and equitable distribution against the other. Each party releases and waives any claims for special equity in the other party's separate property or in jointly owned property. If either party files for divorce, dissolution, alimony, or spousal support unconnected with divorce, separation, or separate maintenance, the parties agree that either shall, in the filing of said proceedings, ask the court to follow the provisions and terms of this premarital agreement and be bound by the terms of this agreement.

16. **ALIMONY.** In the event of divorce or dissolution of marriage proceedings being filed by either party in any state or country, each party forever waives any right to claim or seek any form of alimony or spousal support, attorneys' fees and costs from the other. Any rights concerning distribution of property are otherwise covered by this agreement, and any rights to community property or claims of special equity are waived and released. In the event that a final judgment or decree of divorce or dissolution of marriage is entered for whatever reason, the parties agree that the provisions of this agreement are in complete settlement of all rights to claim or seek any form of financial support, except child support for any living minor children of the parties, from the other.

17. **DISPOSITION UPON DEATH.** Each party consents that his or her estate, or the estate of the other, may be disposed of by will, codicil, or trust, or in the absence of any such instrument, according to the laws of descent and distribution and intestate succession as if the marriage of the parties had not taken place. In either event, the estate shall be free of any claim or demand of inheritance, dower, curtesy, elective share, family allowance, homestead election, right to serve as executor, administrator, or personal representative, or any spousal or other claim given by law, irrespective of the marriage and any law to the contrary. Neither party intends by this agreement to limit or restrict the right to give to, or receive from, the other an inter vivos or testamentary gift. Neither party intends by this agreement to release, waive, or relinquish any devise or bequest left to either by specific provision in the will or codicil of the other, any property voluntarily transferred by the other, any joint

tenancy created by the other, or any right to serve as executor or personal representative of the other's estate if specifically nominated in the other's will or codicil.

18. DEBTS. Neither party shall assume or become responsible for the payment of any pre-existing debts or obligations of the other party because of the marriage. Neither party shall do anything that would cause the debt or obligation of one of them to be a claim, demand, lien, or encumbrance against the property of the other party without the other party's written consent. If a debt or obligation of one party is asserted as a claim or demand against the property of the other without such written consent, the party who is responsible for the debt or obligation shall indemnify the other from the claim or demand, including the indemnified party's costs, expenses, and attorneys' fees.

19. HOMESTEAD. Each party releases any claim, demand, right, or interest that the party may acquire because of the marriage in any real property of the other because of the homestead property provisions of the laws of any state concerning the descent of the property as homestead.

20. FREE AND VOLUNTARY ACT. The parties acknowledge that executing this agreement is a free and voluntary act, and has not been entered into for any reason other than the desire for the furtherance of their relationship in marriage. Each party acknowledges that he or she has had adequate time to fully consider the consequences of signing this agreement, and has not been pressured, threatened, coerced, or unduly influenced to sign this agreement.

21. GOVERNING LAW. This agreement shall be governed by the laws of _____ _____.

22. SEVERABILITY. If any part of this agreement is adjudged invalid, illegal, or unenforceable, the remaining parts shall not be affected.

23. FURTHER ASSURANCE. Each party shall execute any instruments or documents at any time requested by the other party that are necessary or proper to effectuate this agreement.

24. NO OTHER BENEFICIARY. No person shall have a right or cause of action arising or resulting from this agreement except those who are parties to it and their successors in interest.

25. RELEASE. Except as otherwise provided in this agreement, each party releases all claims or demands to the property or estate of the other, however and whenever acquired, including acquisitions in the future.

26. ENTIRE AGREEMENT. This instrument, including any attached exhibits, constitutes the entire agreement of the parties. No representations or promises have been made except those that are set out in this agreement. This agreement may not be modified or terminated except in writing signed by the parties.

27. PARAGRAPH HEADINGS. The headings of the paragraphs contained in this agreement are for convenience only, and are not to be considered a part of this agreement or used in determining its content or context.

28. ATTORNEYS' FEES IN ENFORCEMENT. A party who fails to comply with any provision or obligation contained in this agreement shall pay the other party's attorneys' fees, costs, and other expenses reasonably incurred in enforcing this agreement and resulting from the noncompliance.

29. SIGNATURES AND INITIALS OF PARTIES. The signatures of the parties on this document, and their initials on each page, indicate that each party has read, and agrees with, this entire Premarital Agreement, including any and all exhibits attached hereto. Any provision containing a box, ❑ , which does not contain an "X" does not apply and is not a part of the agreement of the parties.

30. ❑ OTHER PROVISIONS. Additional provisions are contained in the Addendum to Premarital Agreement attached hereto and made a part hereof.

_____   _____
Husband   Wife

Executed in the presence of:

_____   _____
Name:_____   Name:_____
Address:_____   Address:_____
_____   _____

STATE OF   )
COUNTY OF   )

        The foregoing Premarital Agreement, consisting of _____ pages and Exhibits _____ through _____, was acknowledged before me this _____ day of _____, _____, by _____, the above-named Husband, Wife and Witnesses respectively, who are personally known to me or who have produced _____ _____as identification.

_____
Signature

_____
(Typed Name of Acknowledger)
NOTARY PUBLIC
Commission Number:_____
My Commission Expires:

PREMARITAL AGREEMENT

This Agreement is entered into on _____, _____, by and between _____ (hereafter referred to as the Husband), and _____ (hereafter referred to as the Wife), who agree that:

1.   MARRIAGE.

The parties plan to marry each other, and intend to provide in this agreement for their property and other rights that may arise because of their contemplated marriage.

2.   PURPOSE OF AGREEMENT.

❑ (A)   Both parties currently own assets, and anticipate acquiring additional assets, which they wish to continue to control, and are executing this Agreement to establish and determine their respective rights and responsibilities during the marriage, in the event of a divorce or dissolution of the marriage, or the death of one of the parties.

❑ (B)   The parties desire that each party having any child(ren) of a prior marriage be able to identify and maintain a separate estate so as to provide for such child(ren), and each party has the following children of a prior marriage:

❑ Husband:_____.

❑ Wife:_____.

3.   FINANCIAL DISCLOSURE.

❑ (A)   The parties have fully disclosed to each other complete financial information regarding their net worth, assets, holdings, income, and liabilities; both by their discussions with each other, and through their current financial statements, copies of which are attached hereto as Exhibit A and Exhibit B. Both parties acknowledge that they have had sufficient time to review the other's financial statement, are familiar with and understand the other's financial statement, have had any questions satisfactorily answered, and are satisfied that full and complete financial disclosure has been made by the other.

❑ (B) The ❑ Husband ❑ Wife acknowledges that he/she is fully acquainted with the business and resources of the other party; that the other party is a person of substantial wealth; that the other party has answered all questions asked about his/her income and assets; that he/she understands that by entering into this agreement he/she may receive less than he/she would otherwise be entitled to under law in the event of divorce, dissolution of marriage, separation, or death of the other party; that he/she has carefully weighed all facts and circumstances; and that he/she desires to marry the other party regardless of any financial arrangements made for his/her benefit.

4.　ADVICE OF COUNSEL.

❑　(A)　Each party has had advice of independent counsel prior to executing this agreement.
The Husband received such counsel from _____.
The Wife received such counsel from_____.
As a result of such independent counsel, both parties acknowledge that they have been informed of their legal rights in the property currently owned by each of them, rights in any property which may be acquired by either or both of them during their marriage, rights to claim interests in such property, rights to seek alimony upon divorce or dissolution of marriage, rights of inheritance and support as a surviving spouse, rights to take a certain share of the other's estate in the event the other's will makes unacceptable provisions for him or her, and has been informed of the consequences of any waivers, releases and surrenders of such rights pursuant this agreement.

❑　(B)　Each party has had sufficient opportunity to seek advice of independent counsel prior to executing this agreement.

The　❑ Husband　❑ Wife　has received the advice of independent counsel from _____, prior to executing this agreement.

The　❑ Husband　❑ Wife has not sought the advice of independent counsel, despite urging by the other party to do so, and despite being given sufficient time in which to seek such advice.　Such party's failure to consult independent counsel constitutes a waiver of such right.　By signing this agreement, each party acknowledges that he or she understands the terms of this agreement, is aware of his or her legal rights and obligations under this agreement or arising because of their contemplated marriage, and understands the consequences of his or her waivers, releases and surrenders of such rights pursuant to this agreement.

❑　(C)　Each party has had legal and financial advice, or has had the opportunity to consult independent legal and financial counsel, prior to executing this agreement.　Either party's failure to consult legal and financial counsel constitutes a waiver of such right. By signing this agreement, each party acknowledges that he or she understands the terms of this agreement, is aware of his or her legal rights and obligations under this agreement or arising because of their contemplated marriage, and understands the consequences of his or her waivers, releases and surrenders of such rights under this agreement.

5. CONSIDERATION.

The parties acknowledge that each of them would not enter into the contemplated marriage except for the execution of this agreement.

6. EFFECTIVE DATE.

This Agreement shall become effective and binding upon the marriage of the parties. In the event the marriage does not take place, this agreement shall be null and void.

7. DEFINITIONS.

As used in this agreement, the following terms shall have the following meanings:

(a) "Joint Property" means property held and owned by the parties together. Such ownership shall be as tenants by the entirety in jurisdictions where such a tenancy is permitted. If such jurisdiction does not recognize or permit a tenancy by the entirety, then ownership shall be as joint tenants with rights of survivorship. The intention of the parties is to hold joint property as tenants by the entirety whenever possible. "Joint property" also means community property as to any property which may be subject to community property laws.

(b) "Joint Tenancy" means tenancy by the entirety in jurisdictions where such a tenancy is permitted, and joint tenancy with rights of survivorship if tenancy by the entirety is not recognized or permitted. The intention of the parties is to hold joint property as tenants by the entirety whenever possible." Joint property" also refers to community property as to any property which may be subject to community property laws.

(c) "Separate Property" means property owned by either party which is and will remain, or may be acquired, as that party's individual property, free from any claims of the other party. "Separate property" is not part of the community property estate in any state recognizing community property.

8. HUSBAND'S SEPARATE PROPERTY.

The Husband is the owner of certain property, which is set forth and described in Exhibit C attached hereto and made a part hereof, which he intends to keep as his nonmarital, separate, sole, and individual property. All income, rents, profits, interest, dividends, stock splits, gains, and appreciation in value, relating to any such separate property shall also be deemed separate property. All inheritances or gifts received by the Husband individually during the marriage shall also be deemed separate property.

9. WIFE'S SEPARATE PROPERTY.

The Wife is the owner of certain property, which is set forth and described in Exhibit D attached hereto and made a part hereof, which she intends to keep as her nonmarital, separate, sole, and individual property. All income, rents, profits, interest, dividends, stock splits, gains, and appreciation in value, relating to any such separate property shall also be deemed separate property. All inheritances or gifts received by the Wife individually during the marriage shall also be deemed separate property.

10.   JOINT OR COMMUNITY PROPERTY.

The parties intend that certain property shall, from the beginning of the marriage, be joint, as set forth and described in Exhibit E attached hereto and made a part hereof.

11.   PROPERTY ACQUIRED DURING MARRIAGE.

The parties recognize that either or both of them may acquire property during the marriage. The parties agree that the manner in which such property is titled during the marriage shall control such property's ownership and distribution in the event of divorce, dissolution of marriage, separation, or death of either party. Such property shall be held as stated in the instrument conveying or evidencing title. If the instrument does not specify or if there is no instrument, the property shall be held as a tenancy by the entirety, or as a joint tenancy with rights of survivorship in the event tenancy by the entirety is not recognized by the state having jurisdiction over the distribution of such property. Any property acquired that does not normally have a title or ownership certificate shall be considered as joint property unless otherwise specified by the parties in writing. All wedding gifts shall be deemed joint property, unless specified as separate property in either Exhibit C or D.

12.   BANK ACCOUNTS.

Any funds deposited in either party's separate bank accounts shall be deemed that party's separate property. Any funds deposited in a bank account held by the parties jointly shall be deemed joint property.

13.   PAYMENT OF EXPENSES.

The parties agree that their expenses shall be paid as set forth in Exhibit F attached hereto and made a part hereof.

14.   INCOME FROM AND REINVESTMENT OF SEPARATE PROPERTY.

❏ (A) Any property obtained by either party due to the use, investment, reinvestment or any transfer of any portion of his or her separate property, and any income from any such property, and any appreciation in the value of such property, shall remain that party's separate property.

❏ (B) Any property obtained by either party due to the use, investment, reinvestment or any transfer of any portion of his or her separate property, and any income from any such property, shall remain that party's separate property. Any appreciation or other increase in the value of either party's separate property, shall remain that party's separate property, unless the other party has made a direct financial contribution to the increase in value, such as by investing his or her own funds, and then only to the proportion of the increase attributable to his or her investment.

15.   RESIDENCE OF THE PARTIES.

❑ (A) It is expressly recognized that the   ❑ Husband   ❑ Wife is the sole owner of the residence to be occupied by the parties at _____ _____and that the use of any joint funds, or separate funds of the other party, for the mortgage payments, utilities, capital improvements, repair or maintenance of the residence and grounds for the joint benefit of the parties shall not create any interest in the property in the other party.

❑ (B) It is expressly recognized that the   ❑ Husband   ❑ Wife is the sole owner of the residence to be occupied by the parties at _____ _____and that the use of any joint funds, or separate funds of the other party, for the mortgage payments, utilities, repair or maintenance of the residence and grounds for the joint benefit of the parties shall not create any interest in the property in the other party. However, if joint funds or the other party's separate funds are used to make capital improvements on the property, the other party shall thereafter have a lien against the property to the extent of one-half of the total joint funds, or the full amount of the separate funds, contributed, which lien shall be paid upon the sale of the property, the termination of the marriage, or the death of the Husband or Wife, whichever occurs first.

16.   DISPOSITION OF PROPERTY.

Each party retains the ownership, management and control of his or her separate property, and may encumber, sell, or dispose of the property without the other party's consent. Each party shall, on the request of the other, execute any instrument necessary to effectuate this paragraph. The failure ore refusal of a party to join in or execute an instrument required by this paragraph shall entitle the other party to sue for specific performance or for damages, regardless of the doctrine of spousal immunity, and the defaulting party shall pay the other party's costs, expenses and attorneys' fees. This paragraph shall not require a party to execute a promissory note or other evidence of debt for the other party; but if a party executes a promissory note or other evidence of debt for the other party, that other party shall indemnify the party executing the note or other evidence of debt from any claims or demands arising from the execution of the instrument. Execution of an instrument shall not give the executing party any right or interest in the property of the party requesting execution.

17. **PROPERTY DIVISION UPON DIVORCE, DISSOLUTION OF MARRIAGE, OR SEPARATION.**

In the event of divorce, dissolution of marriage, or separation proceedings being filed and pursued by either party, the parties agree that the terms and provisions of this agreement shall govern all of their rights as to property; alimony including permanent periodic, rehabilitative, and lump sum; property settlement; rights of community property; and equitable distribution against the other. Each party releases and waives any claims for special equity in the other party's separate property or in jointly owned property. If either party files for alimony, or spousal support unconnected with divorce, dissolution of marriage, separation, or separate maintenance, the parties agree that the party filing said proceedings shall ask the court to follow the provisions and terms of this premarital agreement.

18. **ALIMONY.**

❑ (A) In the event of divorce or dissolution of marriage proceedings being filed by either party in any state or country, each party forever waives any right to claim or seek any form of alimony or spousal support, and attorneys' fees and costs from the other. Any rights regarding distribution of property are otherwise covered by this agreement, and any rights to community property or claims of special equity are waived and released. In the event that a final judgment or decree of divorce or dissolution of marriage is entered, the parties agree that the provisions of this agreement are in complete settlement of all rights to claim or seek any form of financial support, except child support for any living minor children of the parties, from the other.

❑ (B) In the event divorce, dissolution of marriage, separation, or similar proceedings are filed by either party in any state or country, the parties agree that neither party will request or receive alimony or support, whether temporary, rehabilitative, permanent, or lump sum. In consideration for not requesting alimony, the ❑ Husband ❑ Wife shall pay to the other party a sum equal to $_____ for each full year of marriage up to the date a divorce, dissolution of marriage, separation, or similar action is filed. Said sum shall be paid regardless of which party files, and shall terminate on either the death or remarriage of the payee, or on the death of the payor, whichever occurs first.

❑ (C) In the event of divorce or dissolution of marriage proceedings being filed by either party in any state or country, the ❑ Husband ❑ Wife agrees to pay to the other party temporary and rehabilitative alimony in the sum of $_____ per _____, for a period of _____ years after the date a divorce, dissolution of marriage, or separation action is filed. Said sum shall be paid regardless of which party files, and shall terminate at the end of the period stated above, or on either the death or remarriage of the payee, or on the death of the payor, whichever occurs first.

❏ (D) In the event of divorce or dissolution of marriage proceedings being filed by either party in any state or country, the ❏ Husband ❏ Wife agrees to pay to the other party temporary and permanent periodic alimony in the sum of $_____ per _____. Said sum shall be paid regardless of which party files, and shall terminate on either the death or remarriage of the payee, or on the death of the payor, whichever occurs first.

19. **CHILD SUPPORT.**

In the event of divorce, dissolution of marriage, or separation, and there are any minor children of the parties' marriage, the parties agree that each shall contribute to the support of any such children in the following proportions:

_____% from the Husband.

_____% from the Wife.

Such support shall continue until:

❏ Age 18.

❏ Age 18, or graduation from high school, whichever occurs last, provided any such child is enrolled as a full time student and is making a good faith effort to graduate.

❏ Graduation from college or trade school, provided any such child is enrolled as a full time student and is making a good faith effort to graduate.

❏ The amount of support shall be determined by agreement of the parties. If the parties cannot agree, the amount of support shall be determined by the court. Both parties acknowledge that they are aware that the court has the ultimate authority to determine child support, taking into consideration the needs of the children and any other factors required by law to be considered.

20. **DISPOSITION UPON DEATH.**

❏ (A) Each party consents that his or her estate, or the estate of the other, may be disposed of by will, codicil, or trust, or in the absence of any such instrument, according to the laws of descent and distribution and intestate succession as if the marriage of the parties had not taken place. In either event, the estate shall be free of any claim or demand of inheritance, dower, curtesy, elective share, family allowance, homestead election, right to serve as executor, administrator, or personal representative, or any spousal or other claim given by law, irrespective of the marriage and any law to the contrary. Neither party intends by this agreement to limit or restrict the right to give to, or receive from, the other an inter vivos or testamentary gift. Neither party intends by this agreement to release, waive, or relinquish any devise or bequest left to either by specific provision in the will or codicil of the other, any property voluntarily transferred by the other, any joint tenancy created by the other, or any right to serve as executor or personal representative of the other's estate if specifically nominated in the other's will or codicil.

❏ (B) Subject to the conditions set forth in this paragraph, the ❏ Husband ❏ Wife shall receive and accept from the other party after his/her death, the sum of

$_____, free of any and all inheritance and estate taxes, in place of, and in full and final settlement and satisfaction of, any and all rights and claims which he/she might otherwise have in the other party's estate and property under any law now or hereafter in force in this or any other jurisdiction, whether by way of a right of election to take against the other party's will, as a share of the estate in intestacy, or otherwise. The ❑ Husband ❑ Wife shall only be entitled to receive said amount if all of the following conditions are met: (1) the parties were married at the time of death, (2) he/she survives the decedent, (3) the parties were not separated at the time of death, and (4) no divorce, dissolution of marriage, or separation proceedings were in progress at the time of death. If any of the above conditions are not met, then he/she shall not be entitled to any sums from the other party's estate.

21. **LIFE INSURANCE.**

The parties shall maintain the following life insurance policies payable to the other party on death in the face amounts of at least:

Life insurance on the life of the Husband payable to the Wife or a person she designates of at least $_____.

Life insurance on the life of the Wife payable to the Husband or a person he designates of at least $_____.

22. **DEBTS.**

Neither party shall assume or become responsible for the payment of any preexisting debts or obligations of the other party because of the marriage. Neither party shall do anything that would cause the debt or obligation of one of them to become a claim, demand, lien, or encumbrance on the other's property without the other party's written consent. If a debt or obligation of one party is asserted as a claim or demand against the other's separate property without such written consent, the party who is responsible for the debt or obligation shall indemnify the other from the claim or demand, including the payment of the other party's costs, expenses, and attorneys' fees.

23. **HOMESTEAD.**

Each party releases any claim, demand, right, or interest that the party may acquire because of the marriage in any real property of the other because of the homestead property provisions of the laws of any state concerning the descent of the property as homestead.

24. **COMMINGLING OF INCOME AND ASSETS.**

The parties recognize that it is possible for their income or assets to become, or appear to become, commingled. It is the parties' intention that any commingling of income or assets shall not be interpreted to imply any abandonment of the terms and provisions of this agreement, that the provisions contained herein regarding the parties' interests in jointly held property be applied, and that in other instances each party's interest be determined by each party's proportionate contribution toward the total funds or value of assets in question.

25. **TAX RETURNS / GIFTS / LEGAL PROCEEDINGS.**

The fact that the parties may file joint local, state, or federal income tax returns, or any other joint tax papers or documents, or make gifts of property or cash to each other or not account to each other with regard to the expenditure of income shall not be interpreted to imply any abandonment of the terms and provisions of this agreement. The filing of a divorce, dissolution of marriage, separation, or other legal action or proceeding shall not be deemed as any abandonment of the terms and provisions of this agreement.

26. **FREE AND VOLUNTARY ACT.**

The parties acknowledge that executing this agreement is a free and voluntary act, and has not been entered into for any reason other that the desire for the furtherance of their relationship in marriage. Each party acknowledges that he or she has had adequate time to fully consider the consequences of signing this agreement, and has not been pressured, threatened, coerced, or unduly influenced to sign this agreement.

27. **GOVERNING LAW.**

This agreement shall be governed by the laws of _____.

28. **SEVERABILITY.**

If any part of this agreement is adjudged invalid, illegal, or unenforceable, the remaining parts shall not be affected.

29. **FURTHER ASSURANCE.**

Each party shall execute any instruments or documents at any time requested by the other party that are necessary or proper to effectuate this agreement.

30. **BINDING AGREEMENT / NO OTHER BENEFICIARY.**

This agreement shall be binding upon the parties, and upon their heirs, executors, personal representatives, administrators, and assigns. No person shall have a right or cause of action arising or resulting from this agreement except those who are parties to it and their successors in interest.

31. RELEASE.

Except as otherwise provided in this agreement, each party releases all claims or demands to the property or estate of the other, however and whenever acquired, including acquisitions in the future.

32. ENTIRE AGREEMENT.

This instrument, including any attached exhibits, constitutes the entire agreement of the parties. No representations or promises have been made except those that are set out in this agreement. This agreement may not be modified or terminated except in writing signed by the parties.

33. PARAGRAPH HEADINGS.

The headings of the paragraphs contained in this agreement are for convenience only, and are not to be considered a part of this agreement or used in determining its content or context.

34. ATTORNEYS' FEES IN ENFORCEMENT.

A party who fails to comply with any provision or obligation contained in this agreement shall pay the other party's attorneys' fees, costs, and other expenses reasonably incurred in enforcing this agreement and resulting from the noncompliance.

35. SIGNATURES AND INITIALS OF PARTIES.

The signatures of the parties on this document, and their initials on each page, indicate that each party has read, and agrees with, this entire Premarital Agreement, including any and all exhibits attached hereto. Any provision containing a box, ❑ , which does not contain an "X" does not apply and is not a part of the agreement of the parties.

36. ❑ OTHER PROVISIONS. Additional provisions are contained in the Addendum to Premarital Agreement attached hereto and made a part hereof.

_____   _____
Husband   Wife

Executed in the presence of:

_____   _____
Name:_____   Name:_____
Address:_____   Address:_____
_____   _____

STATE OF   )
COUNTY OF   )

      The foregoing Premarital Agreement, consisting of _____ pages and Exhibits _____ through _____, was acknowledged before me this _____ day of _____, _____, by _____ _____, the above-named Husband, Wife and Witnesses respectively, who are personally known to me or who have produced _____ _____ as identification.

_____

Signature

_____

(Typed Name of Acknowledger)

NOTARY PUBLIC

Commission Number:_____
My Commission Expires:

Husband's Financial Statement

I, _____, hereby certify that the following financial information is true and correct according to the best of my knowledge and belief:

ITEM 1: EMPLOYMENT AND INCOME

OCCUPATION: _____

EMPLOYED BY: _____

ADDRESS: _____

_____

SOC. SEC. #: _____

PAY PERIOD: _____

RATE OF PAY: _____

AVERAGE GROSS MONTHLY INCOME FROM EMPLOYMENT $_____

Bonuses, commissions, allowances, overtime, tips and similar payments   _____

Business Income from sources such as self-employment, partnerships,
       close corporations, and/or independent contracts (gross receipts
       minus ordinary and necessary expenses required to produce income)   _____

Disability benefits   _____

Workers' Compensation   _____

Unemployment Compensation   _____

Pension, retirement, or annuity payments   _____

Social Security benefits   _____

Spousal support received from previous marriage   _____

Interest and dividends   _____

Rental income (gross receipts minus ordinary and necessary expenses
       required to produce income)   _____

Income from royalties, trusts, or estates   _____

Other income of a recurring nature:

_____   _____

_____   _____

_____   _____

     TOTAL GROSS MONTHLY INCOME $_____

LESS DEDUCTIONS:

Federal, state, and local income taxes $_____

FICA or self-employment tax (annualized)   _____

Mandatory union dues   _____

Mandatory retirement   _____

Health insurance payments   _____

Court ordered child support payments (actually paid)   _____

Other deductions:

_____   _____

_____   _____

     -TOTAL DEDUCTIONS $_____

TOTAL NET MONTHLY INCOME $_____

EXHIBIT A

ITEM 2: ASSETS

Description	Value

Cash (on hand or in banks) $_____
Stocks/bonds/notes/annuities/other investments:

_____ _____
_____ _____
_____ _____
_____ _____
_____ _____
_____ _____

Real Estate:

_____ _____
_____ _____
_____ _____
_____ _____

Automobiles:

_____ _____
_____ _____
_____ _____

Boats or other vehicles:

_____ _____
_____ _____
_____ _____

Other personal property:
    Clothing and personal items _____
    Contents of home _____
    Jewelry _____
    Collections (art, coins, stamps, etc.) _____
    Recreation/sports equipment _____
    Trade tools/equipment _____
    Life Insurance (cash surrender value) _____

Business Ownership/Interest:

_____ _____
_____ _____
_____ _____

Other Assets:

_____ _____
_____ _____
_____ _____
_____ _____
_____ _____

TOTAL ASSETS: $_____

ITEM 3: LIABILITIES

Creditor	Security	Balance
_____	_____	$_____
_____	_____	_____
_____	_____	_____
_____	_____	_____
_____	_____	_____
_____	_____	_____
_____	_____	_____
_____	_____	_____
_____	_____	_____
_____	_____	_____
_____	_____	_____
_____	_____	_____
_____	_____	_____
_____	_____	_____
_____	_____	_____
_____	_____	_____
_____	_____	_____
_____	_____	_____

TOTAL LIABILITIES: $_____

The above information is true and accurate to the best of my knowledge, and is based upon information currently available to me. This information is being provided in connection with a Premarital Agreement, and this statement shall be attached to said Premarital Agreement.

DATED:_____   _____
                                 Signature of Husband

ACKNOWLEDGMENT OF RECEIPT

I, _____, hereby acknowledge receiving a copy of the foregoing Husband's Financial Statement on _____, _____.

DATED:_____   _____
                                 Signature of Wife

WIFE'S FINANCIAL STATEMENT

I, _____, hereby certify that the following financial information is true and correct according to the best of my knowledge and belief:

ITEM 1: EMPLOYMENT AND INCOME

OCCUPATION: _____

EMPLOYED BY: _____

ADDRESS: _____

_____

SOC. SEC. #: _____

PAY PERIOD: _____

RATE OF PAY: _____

AVERAGE GROSS MONTHLY INCOME FROM EMPLOYMENT $_____

Bonuses, commissions, allowances, overtime, tips and similar payments   _____

Business Income from sources such as self-employment, partnerships, close corporations, and/or independent contracts (gross receipts minus ordinary and necessary expenses required to produce income)   _____

Disability benefits   _____

Workers' Compensation   _____

Unemployment Compensation   _____

Pension, retirement, or annuity payments   _____

Social Security benefits   _____

Spousal support received from previous marriage   _____

Interest and dividends   _____

Rental income (gross receipts minus ordinary and necessary expenses required to produce income)   _____

Income from royalties, trusts, or estates   _____

Other income of a recurring nature:

_____   _____

_____   _____

_____   _____

     TOTAL GROSS MONTHLY INCOME $_____

LESS DEDUCTIONS:

Federal, state, and local income taxes $_____

FICA or self-employment tax (annualized)   _____

Mandatory union dues   _____

Mandatory retirement   _____

Health insurance payments   _____

Court ordered child support payments (actually paid)   _____

Other deductions:

_____   _____

_____   _____

     -TOTAL DEDUCTIONS $_____

TOTAL NET MONTHLY INCOME $_____

          EXHIBIT B

ITEM 2: ASSETS

Description	Value
Cash (on hand or in banks)	$_____
Stocks/bonds/notes/annuities/other investments:	
_____	_____
_____	_____
_____	_____
_____	_____
_____	_____
_____	_____
Real Estate:	
_____	_____
_____	_____
_____	_____
Automobiles:	
_____	_____
_____	_____
_____	_____
Boats or other vehicles:	
_____	_____
_____	_____
_____	_____
Other personal property:	
Clothing and personal items	_____
Contents of home	_____
Jewelry	_____
Collections (art, coins, stamps, etc.)	_____
Recreation/sports equipment	_____
Trade tools/equipment	_____
Life Insurance (cash surrender value)	_____
Business Ownership/Interest:	
_____	_____
_____	_____
_____	_____
Other Assets:	
_____	_____
_____	_____
_____	_____
_____	_____
_____	_____
TOTAL ASSETS:	$_____

ITEM 3: LIABILITIES

Creditor	Security	Balance
_____	_____	$_____
_____	_____	_____
_____	_____	_____
_____	_____	_____
_____	_____	_____
_____	_____	_____
_____	_____	_____
_____	_____	_____
_____	_____	_____
_____	_____	_____
_____	_____	_____
_____	_____	_____
_____	_____	_____
_____	_____	_____
_____	_____	_____
_____	_____	_____
_____	_____	_____
_____	_____	_____
_____	_____	_____

TOTAL LIABILITIES: $_____

The above information is true and accurate to the best of my knowledge, and is based upon information currently available to me. This information is being provided in connection with a Premarital Agreement, and this statement shall be attached to said Premarital Agreement.

DATED:_____   _____
                                   Signature of Wife

ACKNOWLEDGMENT OF RECEIPT

I, _____, hereby acknowledge receiving a copy of the foregoing Wife's Financial Statement on _____, _____.

DATED:_____   _____
                                   Signature of Husband

HUSBAND'S SCHEDULE OF SEPARATE PROPERTY

This schedule is hereby made a part of the parties' Premarital Agreement, dated _____, _____. The following items of property shall be the separate property of the Husband:

EXHIBIT C

WIFE'S SCHEDULE OF SEPARATE PROPERTY

This schedule is hereby made a part of the parties' Premarital Agreement, dated _____, _____. The following items of property shall be the separate property of the Wife:

EXHIBIT D

Schedule of Joint Property

This schedule is hereby made a part of the parties' Premarital Agreement, dated _____, _____. The following items of property shall be the joint property of the parties:

EXHIBIT E

EXPENSE PAYMENT SCHEDULE

In connection with the Premarital Agreement, dated _____, _____, the parties agree to the following schedule for the manner in which they shall pay for their living expenses:

	HUSBAND	WIFE

HOUSEHOLD:

	HUSBAND	WIFE
Mortgage or rent payments	_____	_____
Property taxes	_____	_____
Homeowners/renters insurance	_____	_____
Electricity	_____	_____
Water & sewer	_____	_____
Garbage collection	_____	_____
Telephone	_____	_____
Fuel oil or natural gas	_____	_____
Repairs and maintenance	_____	_____
Lawn care	_____	_____
Pool care	_____	_____
Pest control	_____	_____
Food and grocery items	_____	_____
Other:		
_____	_____	_____
_____	_____	_____
_____	_____	_____

AUTOMOBILE:

	HUSBAND	WIFE
Gasoline and oil	_____	
Repairs	_____	_____
Auto tags and license	_____	_____
Insurance	_____	_____
Other:		
_____	_____	_____
_____	_____	_____

INSURANCE:

	HUSBAND	WIFE
Health	_____	
Life	_____	_____
Other:		
_____	_____	_____
_____	_____	_____

EXHIBIT F

	HUSBAND	WIFE

OTHER EXPENSES:
Entertainment
Vacations
Pets (veterinarian & grooming, etc.)
Charities
Religious organizations
Other:

_____

_____

_____

_____

_____

CHILDREN'S EXPENSES:
Nursery or babysitting
School tuition
School supplies
Lunch money
Allowance
Clothing
Medical, dental, prescriptions
Vitamins
Barber/beauty parlor
Cosmetics/toiletries
Gifts for special holidays
Other:

_____

_____

_____

_____

Unless otherwise noted above, each party shall be responsible for the payment of the expenses relating to his or her own automobile; children of prior marriages; clothing, personal effects, and grooming expenses; and employment or other career and income producing expenses.

ADDENDUM TO PREMARITAL AGREEMENT

The parties agree to the following terms and conditions, which are in addition to those set forth in their Premarital Agreement dated _____, _____.

AMENDMENT TO PREMARITAL AGREEMENT

This Amendment to Premarital Agreement is entered into on _____, _____, by and between _____ (hereafter referred to as the Husband), and _____ (hereafter referred to as the Wife), who agree that they wish to amend their Premarital Agreement dated _____, _____, as follows:

1.   The parties' Premarital Agreement shall be amended to provide:

2.   In all other respects not referred to herein, said Premarital Agreement is ratified and confirmed, and shall remain in full force and effect.

3.   The parties agree and acknowledge that there has been full and complete disclosure in all respects as if this had been an original Premarital Agreement, and that the parties have each had sufficient opportunity to obtain legal and financial advice from independent counsel prior to signing this Amendment to Premarital Agreement.

_____   _____
Husband   Wife

Executed in the presence of:

_____   _____
Name: _____   Name: _____
Address: _____   Address: _____
        _____   _____

STATE OF   )
COUNTY OF   )

        The foregoing Amendment to Premarital Agreement was acknowledged before me this _____ day of _____, _____, by _____
_____,
the above-named Husband, Wife, and Witnesses respectively, who are personally known to me of who have produced _____
_____ as identification.

_____
Signature

_____
(Typed Name of Acknowledger)

NOTARY PUBLIC

Commission Number: _____
My commission expires:

RELEASE OF PREMARITAL AGREEMENT

This Release of Premarital Agreement is entered into on _____, _____, by and between _____ (hereafter referred to as the Husband), and _____ (hereafter referred to as the Wife), who agree that:

1.   The parties hereby release, cancel, terminate, and set aside in its entirety their Premarital Agreement dated _____, _____, a copy of which is attached hereto.

2.   Any prior transfers of property or rights in property of the parties shall not be affected in any manner by this Release of Premarital Agreement. However, the parties may act separately and independently of this Release of Premarital Agreement to reverse or negate any such prior transfers.

3.   Each party agrees and acknowledges that he or she has had sufficient time to obtain the legal and financial advice of independent counsel, and to consider the consequences of this agreement, prior to signing this Release of Premarital Agreement. Each party further acknowledges and represents that no promises have been made in connection with this Release of Premarital Agreement, except (state any promises, or, if none, state "None"):

4.   The parties agree and acknowledge that there has been full and complete disclosure in all respects as if this had been an original Premarital Agreement.

5.   This Release of Premarital Agreement states the entire agreement between the parties, and may not be modified except in writing signed by both parties before two witnesses and acknowledged by a notary public.

_____   _____
Husband   Wife

Executed in the presence of:

_____   _____
Name:_____   Name:_____
Address:_____   Address:_____
_____   _____

STATE OF)
COUNTY OF)

    The foregoing Release of Premarital Agreement, dated _____,
_____, was acknowledged before me this _____day of_____,_____,by
_____
_____,
the above-named Husband, Wife and Witnesses respectively, who are personally known to
me or who have produced _____
_____as identification.

_____
Signature

_____
(Typed Name of Acknowledger)

NOTARY PUBLIC

Commission Number:_____
My Commission Expires:

INDEX

G

Georgia, 88

H

Hawaii, 23, 89
heir, 72
homestead, 72
How to Win Friends and Influence People, 38

I

Idaho, 90
Illinois, 23, 91
Indiana, 92
In re Marriage of Kesler, 26
intestate, 72
intestate share, 72
Iowa, 23, 93

J

joint property, 9, 29, 63, 72
joint tenancy, 9, 72

K

Kansas, 23, 94
Kentucky, 95

L

law libraries, 32
lawyer referral services, 18
lawyers, *See* attorneys.
legacy, 72
legal encyclopedia, 35
legal research, 32
legatee, 72
life insurance, 60
Louisiana, 96

M

Maine, 23, 97
maintenance, *See* alimony.
marital property, 72
Maryland, 98
Massachusetts, 99
Michigan, 100
military pensions, *See* pensions.
Minnesota, 101
Mississippi, 102
Missouri, 103
Montana, 23, 104

N

Nebraska, 105
Nevada, 23, 106
New Hampshire, 107
New Jersey, 23, 108
New Mexico, 109
New York, 110
nonmarital property, 28, 63, 73
North Carolina, 23, 111
North Dakota, 23, 112
notary public, 42

O

Ohio, 113
Oklahoma, 114
Oregon, 23, 115

P

Pennsylvania, 116
pensions, 31, 64, 65
personal property, 59, 73
personal representative, 73
post-marital agreement, 3, 65
practice manuals, 34
prenuptial agreement, 5, 73
probate, 8, 27
profit-sharing plans, *See* pensions.
property distribution, 11
property division, 5, 6, 8
property ownership, 8

R

real estate, *See* real property.
real property, 58, 73
reporters, case, 34
research, legal, 32
retirement plans, *See* pensions.
revoking an agreement, 70, 130
Rhode Island, 23, 117

S

separate maintenance, *See* alimony.
separate property, *See* nonmarital property.
signing a premarital agreement, 30, 42
sole property, *See* nonmarital property.
South Carolina, 118
South Dakota, 23, 119
state laws,
    in general, 23-35, 75-128
    particular state, *See* name of State.

Your #1 Source for Real World Legal Information...

Sphinx® Publishing
A Division of Sourcebooks, Inc.

- Written by lawyers
- Simple English explanation of the law
- Forms and instructions included

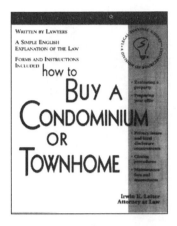

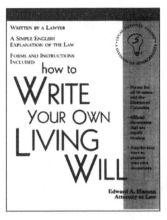

HOW TO BUY A CONDOMINIUM OR TOWNHOME

Provides information on forms of ownership, rights and duties of owners, associations, sample forms and state-by-state listing of statutes.

176 pages; $16.95;
ISBN 1-57071-164-X

HOW TO MAKE YOUR OWN WILL

Valid in 50 states, this book contains 14 different legal forms that will help you put your financial affairs in order. Also discusses inheritance laws.

144 pages; $12.95;
ISBN 1-57071-228-X

HOW TO WRITE YOUR OWN LIVING WILL

Step-by-step guide to writing living wills in all 50 states and the District of Columbia, complete with necessary forms.

160 pages; $9.95;
ISBN 1-57071-167-4

See the following order form for books written specifically for California, Florida, Georgia, Illinois, Massachusetts, Michigan, Minnesota, New York, North Carolina, Pennsylvania, and Texas! *Coming in 1999: Ohio!*

What our customers say about our books:

"It couldn't be more clear for the lay person." —R.D.

"I want you to know I really appreciate your book. It has saved me a lot of time and money." —L.T.

"Your real estate contracts book has saved me nearly $12,000.00 in closing costs over the past year." —A.B.

"...many of the legal questions that I have had over the years were answered clearly and concisely through your plain English interpretation of the law." —C.E.H.

"If there weren't people out there like you I'd be lost. You have the best books of this type out there." —S.B.

"...your forms and directions are easy to follow." —C.V.M.

Sphinx Publishing's Legal Survival Guides
are directly available from the Sourcebooks, Inc., or from your local bookstores.
For credit card orders call 1–800–43-BRIGHT, write P.O. Box 372, Naperville, IL 60566,
or fax 630-961-2168

SPHINX® PUBLISHING NATIONAL TITLES
Valid in All 50 States

LEGAL SURVIVAL IN BUSINESS

How to Form Your Own Corporation (2E)	$19.95
How to Form Your Own Partnership	$19.95
How to Register Your Own Copyright (2E)	$19.95
How to Register Your Own Trademark (2E)	$19.95
Most Valuable Business Legal Forms You'll Ever Need (2E)	$19.95
Most Valuable Corporate Forms You'll Ever Need (2E)	$24.95
Software Law (with diskette)	$29.95

LEGAL SURVIVAL IN COURT

Crime Victim's Guide to Justice	$19.95
Debtors' Rights (3E)	$12.95
Defend Yourself Against Criminal Charges	$19.95
Grandparents' Rights	$19.95
Help Your Lawyer Win Your Case	$12.95
Jurors' Rights (2E)	$9.95
Legal Malpractice and Other Claims Against Your Lawyer	$18.95
Legal Research Made Easy (2E)	$14.95
Simple Ways to Protect Yourself From Lawsuits	$24.95
Victims' Rights	$12.95
Winning Your Personal Injury Claim	$19.95

LEGAL SURVIVAL IN REAL ESTATE

How to Buy a Condominium or Townhome	$16.95
How to Negotiate Real Estate Contracts (3E)	$16.95
How to Negotiate Real Estate Leases (3E)	$16.95
Successful Real Estate Brokerage Management	$19.95

LEGAL SURVIVAL IN PERSONAL AFFAIRS

How to File Your Own Bankruptcy (4E)	$19.95
How to File Your Own Divorce (3E)	$19.95
How to Make Your Own Will	$12.95
How to Write Your Own Living Will	$9.95
How to Write Your Own Premarital Agreement (2E)	$19.95
How to Win Your Unemployment Compensation Claim	$19.95
Living Trusts and Simple Ways to Avoid Probate (2E)	$19.95
Most Valuable Personal Legal Forms You'll Ever Need	$14.95
Neighbor vs. Neighbor	$12.95
The Power of Attorney Handbook (3E)	$19.95
Simple Ways to Protect Yourself from Lawsuits	$24.95
Social Security Benefits Handbook (2E)	$14.95
Unmarried Parents' Rights	$19.95
U.S.A. Immigration Guide (3E)	$19.95
Guia de Inmigracion a Estados Unidos	$19.95

Sphinx Publishing's Legal Survival Guides

are directly available from Sourcebooks, Inc., or from your local bookstores.

For credit card orders call 1–800–43–BRIGHT, write P.O. Box 372, Naperville, IL 60566,
or fax 630-961-2168

SPHINX® PUBLISHING ORDER FORM

BILL TO:			SHIP TO:		
Phone #		Terms	F.O.B.	Chicago, IL	Ship Date

Charge my: ☐ VISA ☐ MasterCard ☐ American Express

☐ **Money Order or Personal Check**

Credit Card Number

Expiration Date

Qty	ISBN	Title	Retail	Ext.
		SPHINX® PUBLISHING NATIONAL TITLES		
	1-57071-166-6	Crime Victim's Guide to Justice	$19.95	
	1-57071-342-1	Debtors' Rights (3E)	$12.95	
	1-57071-162-3	Defend Yourself Against Criminal Charges	$19.95	
	1-57248-001-7	Grandparents' Rights	$19.95	
	0-913825-99-9	Guia de Inmigracion a Estados Unidos	$19.95	
	1-57248-021-1	Help Your Lawyer Win Your Case	$12.95	
	1-57071-164-X	How to Buy a Condominium or Townhome	$16.95	
	1-57071-223-9	How to File Your Own Bankruptcy (4E)	$19.95	
	1-57071-224-7	How to File Your Own Divorce (3E)	$19.95	
	1-57071-227-1	How to Form Your Own Corporation (2E)	$19.95	
	1-57071-343-X	How to Form Your Own Partnership	$19.95	
	1-57071-228-X	How to Make Your Own Will	$12.95	
	1-57071-331-6	How to Negotiate Real Estate Contracts (3E)	$16.95	
	1-57071-332-4	How to Negotiate Real Estate Leases (3E)	$16.95	
	1-57071-225-5	How to Register Your Own Copyright (2E)	$19.95	
	1-57071-226-3	How to Register Your Own Trademark (2E)	$19.95	
	1-57071-349-9	How to Win Your Unemployment Compensation Claim	$19.95	
	1-57071-167-4	How to Write Your Own Living Will	$9.95	
	1-57071-344-8	How to Write Your Own Premarital Agreement (2E)	$19.95	
	1-57071-333-2	Jurors' Rights (2E)	$9.95	
	1-57248-032-7	Legal Malpractice and Other Claims Against...	$18.95	
	1-57071-400-2	Legal Research Made Easy (2E)	$14.95	
	1-57071-336-7	Living Trusts and Simple Ways to Avoid Probate (2E)	$19.95	
	1-57071-345-6	Most Valuable Bus. Legal Forms You'll Ever Need (2E)	$19.95	
	1-57071-346-4	Most Valuable Corporate Forms You'll Ever Need (2E)	$24.95	
	1-57071-347-2	Most Valuable Personal Legal Forms You'll Ever Need	$14.95	

Qty	ISBN	Title	Retail	Ext.
	0-913825-41-7	Neighbor vs. Neighbor	$12.95	
	1-57071-348-0	The Power of Attorney Handbook (3E)	$19.95	
	1-57248-020-3	Simple Ways to Protect Yourself from Lawsuits	$24.95	
	1-57071-337-5	Social Security Benefits Handbook (2E)	$14.95	
	1-57071-163-1	Software Law (w/diskette)	$29.95	
	0-913825-86-7	Successful Real Estate Brokerage Mgmt.	$19.95	
	1-57071-399-5	Unmarried Parents' Rights	$19.95	
	1-57071-354-5	U.S.A. Immigration Guide (3E)	$19.95	
	0-913825-82-4	Victims' Rights	$12.95	
	1-57071-165-8	Winning Your Personal Injury Claim	$19.95	
		CALIFORNIA TITLES		
	1-57071-360-X	CA Power of Attorney Handbook	$12.95	
	1-57071-355-3	How to File for Divorce in CA	$19.95	
	1-57071-356-1	How to Make a CA Will	$12.95	
	1-57071-408-8	How to Probate an Estate in CA	$19.95	
	1-57071-357-X	How to Start a Business in CA	$16.95	
	1-57071-358-8	How to Win in Small Claims Court in CA	$14.95	
	1-57071-359-6	Landlords' Rights and Duties in CA	$19.95	
		FLORIDA TITLES		
	1-57071-363-4	Florida Power of Attorney Handbook (2E)	$9.95	
	1-57071-403-7	How to File for Divorce in FL (5E)	$21.95	
	1-57071-401-0	How to Form a Partnership in FL	$19.95	
	1-57248-004-1	How to Form a Nonprofit Corp. in FL (3E)	$19.95	
	1-57071-380-4	How to Form a Corporation in FL (4E)	$19.95	
	1-57071-361-8	How to Make a FL Will (5E)	$12.95	
		Form Continued on Following Page	**SUBTOTAL**	

To order, call Sourcebooks at 1-800-43-BRIGHT or FAX (630)961-2168 (Bookstores, libraries, wholesalers—please call for discount)

SPHINX® PUBLISHING ORDER FORM

Qty	ISBN	Title	Retail	Ext.
		FLORIDA TITLES (CONT'D)		
____	1-57248-056-4	How to Modify Your FL Divorce Judgement (3E)	$22.95	____
____	1-57071-364-2	How to Probate an Estate in FL (3E)	$24.95	____
____	1-57248-005-X	How to Start a Business in FL (4E)	$16.95	____
____	1-57071-362-6	How to Win in Small Claims Court in FL (6E)	$14.95	____
____	1-57071-335-9	Landlords' Rights and Duties in FL (7E)	$19.95	____
____	1-57071-334-0	Land Trusts in FL (5E)	$24.95	____
____	0-913825-73-5	Women's Legal Rights in FL	$19.95	____
		GEORGIA TITLES		
____	1-57071-387-1	How to File for Divorce in GA (3E)	$19.95	____
____	1-57248-047-5	How to Make a GA Will (2E)	$9.95	____
____	1-57248-026-2	How to Start and Run a GA Business (2E)	$18.95	____
		ILLINOIS TITLES		
____	1-57071-405-3	How to File for Divorce in IL (2E)	$19.95	____
____	1-57071-415-0	How to Make an IL Will (2E)	$12.95	____
____	1-57071-416-9	How to Start a Business in IL (2E)	$16.95	____
		MASSACHUSETTS TITLES		
____	1-57071-329-4	How to File for Divorce in MA (2E)	$19.95	____
____	1-57248-050-5	How to Make a MA Will	$9.95	____
____	1-57248-053-X	How to Probate an Estate in MA	$19.95	____
____	1-57248-054-8	How to Start a Business in MA	$16.95	____
____	1-57248-055-6	Landlords' Rights and Duties in MA	$19.95	____
		MICHIGAN TITLES		
____	1-57071-409-6	How to File for Divorce in MI (2E)	$19.95	____
____	1-57248-015-7	How to Make a MI Will	$9.95	____
____	1-57071-407-X	How to Start a Business in MI (2E)	$16.95	____
		MINNESOTA TITLES		
____	1-57248-039-4	How to File for Divorce in MN	$19.95	____
____	1-57248-040-8	How to Form a Simple Corporation in MN	$19.95	____
____	1-57248-037-8	How to Make a MN Will	$9.95	____
____	1-57248-038-6	How to Start a Business in MN	$16.95	____

Qty	ISBN	Title	Retail	Ext.
		NEW YORK TITLES		
____	1-57071-184-4	How to File for Divorce in NY	$19.95	____
____	1-57071-183-6	How to Make a NY Will	$12.95	____
____	1-57071-185-2	How to Start a Business in NY	$16.95	____
____	1-57071-187-9	How to Win in Small Claims Court in NY	$14.95	____
____	1-57071-186-0	Landlords' Rights and Duties in NY	$19.95	____
____	1-57071-188-7	New York Power of Attorney Handbook	$19.95	____
		NORTH CAROLINA TITLES		
____	1-57071-326-X	How to File for Divorce in NC (2E)	$19.95	____
____	1-57071-327-8	How to Make a NC Will (2E)	$12.95	____
____	0-913825-93-X	How to Start a Business in NC	$16.95	____
		PENNSYLVANIA TITLES		
____	1-57071-177-1	How to File for Divorce in PA	$19.95	____
____	1-57071-176-3	How to Make a PA Will	$12.95	____
____	1-57071-178-X	How to Start a Business in PA	$16.95	____
____	1-57071-179-8	Landlords' Rights and Duties in PA	$19.95	____
		TEXAS TITLES		
____	1-57071-330-8	How to File for Divorce in TX (2E)	$19.95	____
____	1-57248-009-2	How to Form a Simple Corporation in TX	$19.95	____
____	1-57071-417-7	How to Make a TX Will (2E)	$12.95	____
____	1-57071-418-5	How to Probate an Estate in TX (2E)	$19.95	____
____	1-57071-365-0	How to Start a Business in TX (2E)	$16.95	____
____	1-57248-012-2	How to Win in Small Claims Court in TX	$14.95	____
____	1-57248-011-4	Landlords' Rights and Duties in TX	$19.95	____

SUBTOTAL THIS PAGE ____

SUBTOTAL PREVIOUS PAGE ____

Illinois residents add 6.75% sales tax
Florida residents add 6% state sales tax plus applicable discretionary surtax ____

Shipping— $4.00 for 1st book, $1.00 each additional ____

TOTAL ____